Hospice, Humor, Music *and* *More*

A Volunteer's Perspective

JACK E. KILE

www.jackkile.com

ISBN-10: 1463727542
EAN-13: 9781463727543

Dedication

This book is dedicated to the hospice patients and families that I have served over my six years as a volunteer. They have blessed my life in so many ways and taught me much about the passion for living and the preparation for dying.

Contents

Foreword

In 1966, I accepted a teaching position at the University of Wisconsin-Oshkosh along with a young, enthusiastic instructor named Jack Kile. I had no idea how well I would get to know Jack and how much respect I would develop for him over the next 45 years. Never have I met a man with greater compassion for people. He spares nothing to improve the lives of those who are fortunate to enter his world.

The first few years we worked together, my office was adjacent to his. I soon became impressed with the time he spent past working hours teaching people, who had lost their voice boxes (larynges), usually because of cancer, to regain their speech. Not only did I notice his attraction to older folks, especially those with afflictions, but also to children. For example, he had the skill to administer valid hearing tests to infants long before they developed their ability to utter recognizable words. He was so popular with my own two children that I began calling him, "Uncle Jack," which I affectionately continue to do so today.

I retired before Jack and got into hospice volunteering before he did. I happened to be in the group of volunteers one day when Jack and his barbershop quartet entertained us. At that time, he learned about the nature and importance of hospice volunteering. I sometimes claim that my greatest achievement as a hospice volunteer was to introduce Jack to the program, given the number of quality years he's given to it.

Most of us experience natural feelings of sadness and negativity in the death and dying of loved ones. While not denying this phenomenon, Jack invites us to look at the other side of the coin by seeking out positive and happy thoughts by means of caring, humor and song. One of the most difficult events of my life was the night of the visitation for my beloved wife. However, when Jack entered the room and began reviewing pleasant experiences from the past about my family, the feeling in the room turned remarkably more positive and was uplifting.

As you read the detailed accounts of Jack's interactions with patients and families, you sense how an empathetic, caring person can use humor and song to uplift spirits and promote a more positive approach as loved ones pass from this earth to the eternal. You don't have to be a hospice volunteer to learn from this book. It is an inspirational source of information helpful to any of us dealing with end-of-life situations.

S. Clay Wilmington, Ph.D.
Professor Emeritus - Speech Education
University of Wisconsin-Oshkosh

Preface

In the summer of 2005, my barbershop quartet, appropriately named the "4-Bits of Fun," provided entertainment for a hospice volunteer appreciation dinner. As we finished the performance, I commended the volunteers for making a difference in people's lives and as a recent retiree, with professional experience to serve people with illness and disabilities, expressed an interest to join them. I subsequently took the training course that included a tour of a local hospice home. As I toured the Home, I felt uplifted and shortly thereafter became a volunteer. I quickly adapted to the philosophy that gets patients to focus on living and to recognize opportunities to have fun and enjoy life.

My hospice work has been a real blessing for me. I'm passionate about the experience and receive more from it than I give. I often encourage others to get involved and enjoy serving on panels at volunteer training sessions.

Several years ago, I started to give speeches on my hospice work, as it relates to humor and song, to service clubs and to church, retirement and volunteer groups. Their positive responses gave me encouragement to put my thoughts on paper and the idea to write a book evolved.

Early in the preparation of the book, I informed the hospice staff and volunteers of the challenge before me. For the record, I readily acknowledged two things that worked against me: (1). I didn't know anything, and (2). I couldn't write. However, I remained undaunted, and felt an inner confidence. I don't know why. Maybe it was because of the truly remarkable people with whom I worked. They had incredible insights that they shared and gave me encouragement to take on the task.

When I commented to my wife of 49 years, that it hardly seemed possible I had been retired for nine years, she responded that it seemed like an eternity. Often people ask what I have been doing in my retirement years, I quickly respond, "I drive my wife crazy," which draws little argument from her. I recently received an email entitled "A Retiree's Thought," that hit home. It goes like this. My wife said, "What are you doing today?" I said, "Nothing." She said, "You did that yesterday." I said, "I wasn't finished."

To write the book was a good idea for it kept me occupied, although my wife got tired of reviewing every segment and being coerced to give compliments. The preparation of the book has been both a fun and humbling experience, and I've learned a great deal in the process. I hope it's a meaningful read.

Acknowledgements

Special thanks are extended to Dr. Don Derozier, Todd Kile, Dyann Kostello, Ron LaPoint, Chris and Lynn Litzau, Chuck and Toni Palmer, Sister Anne J. Van Lanen and Tina Williamson for their thorough reviews during different stages of the book's development, and also to Linda Becker, Debra Bohrer, Sister Jean Braun, Diane Colwin, Elmer Deitte, Marilyn Drake, Donna Gagne, Pastor Bob Herder, Shirley Karls, Tammy Kile, Mary Nellis, Pastor Bob Rosenberg and Cathy Wolfe for their input.

I'm most grateful to my wife Carol for her support, patience and tolerance during the two year undertaking and to my children (Tammy, Toni and Todd) and son-in-law Chuck for their help and encouragement through my impatience and obsessive behavior. They're the best.

I've learned so much from hospice staff and volunteers whose insights have been invaluable in my growth as a volunteer and in the preparation of this book. I'm very grateful.

Introduction

In my 35 years as a university teacher and clinical audiologist, I was responsible for a hearing clinic that served as a practicum site for my students. I worked with individuals of all ages that included some with multiple disabilities and life-threatening conditions.

Since childhood, I have sought opportunities to have fun and make people laugh. Laughter suggests a sense of contentment, promotes rapport and encourages communication. In my professional career, I found humor and caring to be compatible.

To know when to use humor requires an intuitive sense, as does the evaluation of its effects. You only use it with people you like and for whom you care.

I chose volunteer work to give back to the community in my retirement years. It was important that I feel comfortable with the work and that it fit my experience, personality and interests. In short, I needed to be myself. Before I made a commitment as a hospice volunteer, I did a self-evaluation to determine goodness of fit. Could

I convey happy thoughts and humor with patients and their families without giving the appearance of being disrespectful? I thought I could and still do after six years as a volunteer. In his classic book, *The Power of Positive Thinking*, Dr. Norman Vincent Peale states, "If there is no fun in it, something is wrong with all you're doing." My hospice experience is generally fun, and I receive personal satisfaction from the experience. Many friends thought I would have difficulty making the transition to retirement. However, I found the caring and compassion I had for people in my professional life easily transferred to the lives of my hospice patients and their families.

While this book deals primarily with terminal illness, one cannot underestimate the impact that even the mildest form of health disorder can have on the patient and family. Many years ago, my oldest grandson developed a middle ear infection, a common affliction in small children that responds well to treatment. As an audiologist, I saw many of these "so-called" routine cases. However, when he acquired an ear infection, it was a stressful condition for our family. I instantly became a concerned grandfather and was no longer an audiologist who talked about a routine hearing problem. From this experience, I learned the importance to compassionately care for all patients and families irrespective of their health condition and was reminded, "PEOPLE DON'T CARE HOW MUCH YOU KNOW UNTIL THEY KNOW HOW MUCH YOU CARE."

When one reaches the senior years, there is often a better appreciation of life. As a recent septuagenarian (sixty-nine seemed so much younger), that holds true for me. However, regardless of age, "to make every day count" is a good ingredient for living. For those with terminal illness, the compromised life takes on a different meaning. Some people become sullen and morose while others maintain a zest for life and sense of humor that complement their hospice care. In the book, I accentuate these latter qualities as I talk about patients.

The book, based on my experiences as a hospice volunteer, shows how humor interspersed with song, relates to compassionate caring as one communicates and forms connections with patients and their families.

I've organized the work into five parts and 11 chapters. Part 1 (three chapters) provides a rationale for the use of humor with hospice patients and how to adapt communication (considering physical and mental limitations) to promote humor. It also describes the positive aspects of humor, both physically and psychologically, as related to the emotional needs of patients. Part 2 (two chapters) discusses different types of humor, with an emphasis on my self-deprecating type and how it's used in conversation with patients. In Part 3 (one chapter), I share my love of music and song to create nostalgic moments and to bring back happy memories. Part 4 (four chapters) describes a series of patient stories that are humorous and heart-rending. These vignettes (the heart of the book) offer suggestions for eliminating communication barriers and for creating happy moments. In addition, some isolated stories about hospice patients reveal unexpected humor. Part 5 (one chapter) suggests humor in bereavement based on hospice experience and involvement with my family.

PART 1
Rationale for Humor and its Implementation

CHAPTER 1

Hospice and Humor:
A Conflict?

The philosophy of Hospice recognizes dying as a part of the normal process of living and maximizes the quality of life that remains. Hospice represents compassionate caring and love for patients and families and allows them to develop a mental and spiritual preparation for death.

Palliative care, an important part of hospice services, does not hasten or prolong life or provide a cure for disease, but rather it relieves pain and provides comfort. It's often difficult for the patient and family to adopt a different mind-set and make the transition to hospice care. They are no longer involved with aggressive medical intervention to provide a cure or prolong life. When there is acceptance that death is imminent, family and friends can engage themselves to maximize the quality of life of their loved one.

While illness takes a toll on the person's physical condition, spirit and passion for life and sense of humor often remain intact. Hospice recognizes humor is compatible with its philosophy and its website (www.thehospiceweb-site.com/features/humor.htm) provides links to other sites that encourage people to share humorous experiences they've had with patients. In a Google search, a multitude of references suggests humor to be an effective part of palliative care. More home care providers, hospice staff and volunteers use humor to provide comfort and encouragement to patients and their families.

In spite of the increased acceptance of humor in hospice programs, some still feel its use is inappropriate for those with serious illness. To relate, once when asked to speak at a hospice fundraiser, I suggested the title, "Hospice and Humor." However, the sponsors expressed reluctance for the topic and gave the impression humor was not suitable for these people. Often there is the assumption that sadness, associated with ill health, entails a denial of humor. To the contrary, Allen Klein, in his book, *The Courage to Laugh,* suggests humor is a natural part of life regardless of health. Further, it has dignity and deserves respect. It promotes normalcy to those with illness and encourages communication with others. Often the zeal for life never leaves in spite of terminal illness.

In his book *Humor of Christ,* Elton Trueblood reports that elements in contrast, such as sadness and humor, are often complementary. While crying is associated with sadness, it can also result from humor. How often have you heard or experienced laughter that results in tears?

Erma Bombeck, in her book, *I Want to Grow Hair, I Want to Grow Up, I Want to Go to Boise,* reports initial apprehensiveness about the use of humor with young cancer patients. That is until one of the kids she met said, "Would you be happier if we cried all the time?" She soon realized that these gutsy children had an eternal optimism, laughter and love of life waiting to be developed. A 16-year old boy related how people felt uncomfortable around him. They felt sorry for him and kept the conversation serious. When confronted about his outlook on life, he stated, "Without a sense of humor, I would never have made it this far." From Bombeck, "Laughter rises out of tragedy when you need it the most and rewards you for your courage."

Recently, I read Art Buchwald's book, *Too Soon to Say Goodbye.* Buchwald suffered from multiple health problems that included renal failure. He rejected the thought to have dialysis and decided to spend his final days in a hospice home. The well-known humorist wrote his final book while a hospice patient. The book reflects Buchwald's love for life and "undying" sense of humor. This includes a dream about his flight to heaven only to have it cancelled and he ponders stand-by status. Even with terminal illness, Buchwald continues his journey in life with all the passion and fervor he can muster. He states, "I can't be concerned about dying because I'm too dammed busy living!"

In the movie "The Bucket List," Jack Nicholson and Morgan Freeman, who have terminal illnesses, meet in the hospital as roommates. Nicholson is a billionaire and Freeman has modest means. They develop a bond and friendship. Rather than sit back and wait to die, Nicholson persuades Freeman to share bigger-than-life experiences and do all the things they ever wanted to do. For the next few months, they spare no expense to fulfill their dreams as they do outrageous things and, in the process, have the time of their lives.

In his best-selling book *The Last Lecture*, Dr. Randy Pausch, a computer science professor, who specialized in virtual reality at Carnegie Melton University, talks openly about his terminal illness. He has pancreatic cancer with a prognosis of 6-months to live, but still has fun. He accepts his fate, and while not able to change the cards dealt him, focuses on how to play the hand. For him, anger is not in the cards. When asked in an interview with Diane Sawyer of "Primetime," how he felt, he smiled and said, "I am alive, so I feel great."

As he began his final lecture, "Really Achieving Your Childhood Dreams," Pausch describes the cancer that would soon take his life. Then, with a smile, drops to the floor and does a series of push-ups in rapid succession. In a flash, he changes the audience's mood from one of somber to delight. He talks about one of his earliest childhood dreams to be the coolest guy in an amusement park. That person is the one who struts around the grounds as he carries a large stuffed animal. Through the years, Pausch wins a sizeable number of the toy critters from games on the midway. Before his final lecture, he places many of the prizes on the stage for all to see and offers them to any takers. What a neat way for a brilliant man to share a simple dream. In contrast to Nicholson and Freeman, Pausch's "bucket list" consisted of little moments around the house with his wife and children.

Reportedly, the positive aspects of humor can have a therapeutic effect on those with illness. Humor has a positive impact on life. It builds togetherness and reduces stress. In her book *A Burden Shared*, Jane Kirkpatrick, with poetic prose and compassionate caring, offers encouragement and support for those with burdens. Insightfully, she says, "I want to give you words of joy, spoken to make your spirit laugh and see the brightness of a future filled with those who care." From Mark Twain, "Humor is mankind's greatest blessing." Noted author and humorist, Andy Rooney suggests that a sense of humor is "one of the most universally admired qualities a person can have." Sam Erwin, in his book, *Humor of a Country Lawyer*, reflects: "Humor is one of God's marvelous gifts. Humor gives us smiles, laughter, and gaiety. Humor reveals the roses and hides the thorns. Humor makes our heavy

burdens light and smoothes the rough spots in our path-
ways. Humor endows us with the capacity to clarify the
obscure, to simplify the complex, to deflate the pompous,
to chastise the arrogant, to point a moral, and to adorn a
tale."

Thus, there is strong evidence to suggest that the ju-
dicious use of humor is compatible with the hospice philosophy. For those volunteers who feel comfortable to use
humor, it represents another dimension of patient contact
that creates positive feelings and promotes good will.

CHAPTER 2

Adapting Communication to Promote Humor

While some hospice patients have the potential for humor, communication barriers make it problematic. Some no longer have the cognitive skills to grasp the subtleties of language. Others require time to process what they have heard. My professional experience in communicative disorders has been helpful as I converse with hospice patients. Some communicate effectively throughout illness. Others have speech and/or language disorders. The incidence of hearing impairment is high in older adults. Sometimes it's difficult to determine whether confusion is due to hearing impairment alone or in combination with neurological deficits.

(Often, the hearing impairment in older adults reduces the loudness and clarity for speech. Typically, the hearing loss affects the higher frequencies and distorts speech sounds important to intelligibility. Generally, the troublesome sounds are those consonants (e.g., /f/, /s/, /th/, /sh/, /ch/, /p/, /t/, /k/, /h/) that require high frequency cues for identification. Often these individuals profit from hearing aids and other amplification devices (e.g., pocket amplifiers). With the benefit of amplification, they hear considerably better. However, auditory speech discrimination problems often persist and become more severe when there are noisy backgrounds such as in group listening situations. These people can best utilize auditory and visual clues when spoken to from short distances (<3 feet) at conversational levels.)

As health deteriorates, physical appearance reflects illness and disability. However, intellect and ability to function do not necessarily correlate with physical appearance. To illustrate, I have a good friend with cerebral palsy. He lacks muscle function to control limb movements and walks with an unsteady gate. His speech is slow and labored and some think he is developmentally disabled. Yet, he has a brilliant mind, two college degrees and a wonderful sense of humor. Other patients exhibit listless and lethargic behaviors that compromise communication.

One can often observe alertness in nonverbal patients as you watch their eyes and facial expressions. It requires an intuitive sense. Is there a brightness and sparkle in their eyes? Do they visually track and focus as you speak? Do they smile and display emotion?

I recall a toddler with cerebral palsy whose hearing I evaluated. While he was unable to control the movements of his arms, legs, head and neck, he was visually alert, had a glow in his eyes and possessed a beautiful smile. I sensed he maximized what he could absorb visually. It turned out he had normal intelligence (probably above average) but possessed deafness and a body unable to perform most motor tasks.

Nonverbal exchange is an effective precursor to speech. It is helpful to form connections and to show you care. A powerful form is a smile. This display of positive emotion can result in mood shifts and create happiness. In an instant, a look of gloom and despair can change to a happy face—what a marvelous transformation. In the Dalai Lama's book, *Words of Wisdom,* he states, "The more we care for the happiness of others, the greater our own sense of well-being becomes."

Once when I visited friends at their home, a wall hanging caught my attention. It was an art print by Charlene Winter Olson with the quote, "Every new day is a gift. That's why we call it the present." The words reminded me of an attitude common in many hospice patients who, in spite of compromised lives, still make the most of every day. They still want to be happy. Humor from family and friends helps promote positive relationships.

In his writings, noted theologian Frederick Faber states, "There are souls in this world who have the gift of finding joy everywhere and leaving it behind when they go." I admire people with special gifts who bring happiness to others. Sister Sue, a founder of the Home, is such a person. She has a marvelous presence and celestial smile that breaks through barriers. She breathes new life in the patients and families she serves. Some time ago, I observed a patient and spouse as they ate dinner. Both were in a morose state and gloom-and-doom prevailed. As Sister entered the room, she approached the couple with a warm smile and gentle hug. Immediately, smiles replaced sullen looks and a pleasant conversation followed.

Some hospice patients acquire speech and/or language disorders because of strokes, brain tumors, or other neurological insults. They may hear and understand but have delayed responses. Such was the case of Sam who had an inoperable brain tumor. When I would ask simple questions, it took several seconds to process what he heard. When he retrieved appropriate words to convey thoughts, he spoke with clarity and understanding. I soon realized the wait for Sam to speak was an important communication tool and that his dialogue revealed a delightful sense of humor. We would often joke about who was the better athlete in his prime.

While some patients comprehend the spoken word, it is difficult for them to select appropriate words in their speech. They know when they say wrong words, but are unable to retrieve the right ones to convey thoughts and become frustrated. I have lunch every week with my good friend Jake who had a stroke several years ago. He possesses communication problems that afflict many hospice patients. Fortunately, he is ambulatory and in good physical condition. He always greets me with a smile and hug. Although he struggles to retrieve target words, he perseveres until he makes a point—sometimes with gestures and body language. Some days his speech comes easier and conversation flows. Other times, Jake's conversation is fragmented and difficult to follow. I try to be a patient listener and ask pertinent questions to keep him engaged in the dialogue.

In spite of communication barriers, Jake remains interested in the world and people around him. He is an eternal optimist, and always thankful for what he has. As he says, "I can do a lot of things;" and he can. I have never heard him say a cross word about anyone. **It's as if he thinks, since words don't come easy, why waste them on negative thoughts**. His standard statement when he talks about family and friends is, "He/she is a good person." Jake has a terrific sense of humor and loves to hear a good story. He jokes with the waitress and playfully argues whether it is his or my turn to pay the bill. I usually lose. As I tease him, he grins, shakes his head in disbelief and says, "You've got problems!" Unfortunately, some friends no longer come to see him because of perceived communication barriers. For those that do visit, there is often a reluctance to use humor. Nonetheless, Jake remains upbeat and positive.

As health continues to fail, some patients lose the ability to speak. In some instances, the vocal system is no longer functional as in cases of amyotrophic lateral sclerosis (ALS—Lou Gehrig's disease). As patients struggle to speak, they often try to communicate on paper. However, so much time elapses as one writes the message and poor legibility can deter communication. Often the conversation loses its spontaneity and frame of reference. The use of picture communication boards can identify patient needs and computer driven assistive technology can help nonverbal people when they have the motor and cognitive skills to utilize it.

When I communicate with nonverbal patients, I bring up subjects of interest (e.g., family, hobbies, sports, current events) and look for responses that they can perform (e.g., eye blinks, head movements, facial mannerisms). Often, I'll initiate conversation with questions that elicit "Yes" or "No" answers. One eye blink or an up-and-down movement of the head might be "Yes" and two eye blinks or a head movement from side-to-side "No." I like to tell a joke or story and am pleased when smiles occur.

On occasion, communication modifications occur that go beyond the expected and can have a funny twist. To illustrate, one of my patients with ALS kicked me as a form of communication and I had the bruises to show for her actions. She had a great sense of humor and we had fun as we interacted, at least most of the time.

Sometimes unexpected communication happens as death draws near. Another volunteer and I had a remarkable experience with a woman near death in a semi-comatose state. In a lucid moment, she related a humorous incident I had with her from a previous visit. Another patient, in a similar state, responded with a spiritual encounter. Even when the patient is no longer aware of a volunteer's presence, the family is. They are grateful for the caring and support, and appreciate attempts to remain connected with their loved one.

CHAPTER 3

The Use of Humor with Hospice Patients

The philosopher Soren Kierkegaard recognizes a connection between humor and a childlike behavior that is consistent with maturity. That seems to fit me. I am still a kid at heart. The use of humor is not for everyone and that's okay. Some of the best hospice volunteers are reluctant to use it. Neuroscientist Robert Provine reports most conversational laughter is not the result of structured attempts at humor. Importantly, the use of humor is best when it occurs naturally and spontaneously. Entertainer Steve Allen suggests, "Nothing is quite as funny as the unintended humor of reality."

Sometimes humor takes place without intent and the surprise of it brings relief in an anxious moment. My mother-in-law, ravaged by Alzheimer's disease, saw humor in an incident that others (including my wife) did not deem funny. With her beloved husband hospitalized, she was not a happy camper and was in a cantankerous state. While she no longer understood the scope of their relationship, she knew he was special and missed him dearly.

My wife tried to calm her mother. Once she built a fire in the fireplace at her parent's apartment. However, she miscalculated the status of the chimney's flue. As smoke filled the apartment, my wife, in a panic, opened the windows and waved her arms to extricate the vapor. As her mother observed the escapade, her mood changed suddenly and she laughed hysterically. My wife no longer frustrated by the mishap, enjoyed the humorous moment with her beloved mother.

When to try humor requires one's best judgment. Some patients don't want to be humored. They have a terminal illness, and are not happy away from home. Understandably, they are bitter towards life and angry with everyone.

I once greeted a patient with a cheery "Hello" as we crossed paths and stopped to talk. His response to me was, "Keep walking and talk to someone else." I smiled politely and kept on with my walk. I did not take the remarks to heart for he had good reason not to socialize. He had just lost his last vestige of independence—to take walks around the grounds of the Home. He had become less steady on his feet and now needed assistance. This devastated him. He did not relish the thought to be dependent on others for ALL needs.

This incident brought back memories of my father-in-law who lost his independence as macular degeneration took his sight and congestive heart failure took his health. His body wore out. First, he surrendered his driver's license and next gave up his beloved card game—"bridge." With the sudden dependency on others, he became downcast and morose. However, he adjusted in time, accepted the condition and utilized a sharp mind that he never lost. His sense of humor returned and to tease his favorite and only son-in-law again became a priority. I shouldered the abuse as he made up for lost time.

As relationships develop with hospice patients, there is often a window of opportunity to get them to smile and have fun. While this behavior might occur for a short period, it is well worth the effort, and they will like you for it. As Jay Leno once said, "You can't stay mad at somebody who makes you laugh."

Generally, onsets of a smile and/or laughter are the byproducts of humor. However, as people get older, there is not always an outward display of joy and happiness. My barbershop quartets do a number of sing-outs for senior groups. When we do our comedy routines, we scan the audience to look for feedback. To our dismay, sometimes we observe somber faces and little display of emotion. Smiles and laughter become the exception and not the rule. To our surprise, people often comment how much they enjoyed our performance and how funny we were; so the absence of laughter does not preclude humor. Based on these experiences, we are not too quick to evaluate performances based on outward appearances. I believe there are inner smiles that people enjoy privately. I take these factors in consideration when I use humor with hospice patients.

There is a relationship between health status and laughter. Some patients no longer have the physical/motor mechanisms to generate robust laughter (e.g., ALS, nuclear palsy). When they do react to humor, it might be difficult to suppress aggressive laughter that can exceed the physiological limits of their vocal systems. Others learn to give relaxed smiles as responses to humor. Some patients have the mechanisms to produce laughter but lack the cognitive ability to understand humor.

However, a person's health status or cognitive level should not preclude attempts at humor. One can evaluate the merits and appropriateness based on family input, behavioral observations and innate insights.

In this age of political correctness, the type of humor utilized is critical. My humor tends to poke fun at my own ineptitudes. My flaws might not be funny to the patient but are not offensive. Humor that might compromise the volunteer's credibility is not worth the risk.

While patient and family converse, sometimes others (e.g., volunteers and staff) catch fragments of the conversation and things may not be as they seem. Recently, an incident occurred that tested the appropriateness of humor. Another volunteer and I visited the husband and son of a patient who was in a comatose state. In these situations, I offer support and let the family know I care and try to be a good listener. In this case, I gently stroked the hand of the dying woman and comforted the family. However, as we shared experiences, humor surfaced.

For some reason, the topic turned to food. As we talked, I related a humorous incident about a hospice patient who preferred carryout food from a local restaurant, at my expense, to the cuisine at the hospice residence. After I finished the story, I invited the husband and son to have lunch on-site. Both broke out into laughter as they requested eats from a local restaurant—deja vu. The spontaneous humor got their minds on fun things and a brief respite from stress.

As the room abounded with laughter, a nurse's aide abruptly entered the room. While she didn't utter a word, she gave a stern look in our direction that gave the impression our behavior was inappropriate and in poor taste. I can understand why, for here was a patient close to death, and we were engaged in laughter. While the staff member was not present to observe what had previously transpired, she had the patient and family's best interests at heart. However, under the circumstances, the family thought the humor appropriate. So did I.

Positive Aspects of Humor

So much of what the terminally ill patient deals with is negative and there is little to cheer about. Such is not the case when one engages in wholesome humor and looks for the light side of life. These positive qualities encourage smiles. One of my patient's asked, "What costs the least and does the most?" She responded, "A smile." She then displayed a greeting card from a close friend which said, "I'm sending you a smile to help pick up your day. Let me know if it wears out and I'll send you another." It worked.

It has been said that "Laughter is God's sunshine and music of the soul." During these brief moments, the patient is relaxed, feels good all over and not consumed by physical condition. Furthermore, there is an absence of mood shifts and anxiety is on-hold. Conversation thrives, and there is more interaction with family and friends.

The use of humor can make activities of daily life easier and less stressful. The ability to eat (e.g., chewing, swallowing), often affected by illness, can occur with less effort when patients are relaxed and in a positive frame of mind. Before I feed patients, I often sing a happy song and/or share some humorous stories. They often enjoy the pre-dining experience and look forward to the meal.

Humor promotes conversation. Mark Twain states, "The human race has only one effective weapon and that's laughter. The moment it arises all our hardness's yield, all our irritations and resentments slip away, and a sunny spirit takes their place." Sometimes a joke conjures up memories of a related caper that makes the story even funnier. The person, who hears the story, reels off a favorite story and the fun begins. Did you ever notice at a gathering when there is little activity, things really pick up when someone tells a joke. That opens the door for others to share humorous stories and have a good laugh. If you take a chance to use humor, soon everyone is involved in the conversation and what once was a dull get-together becomes a fun one. This creates a forum to have fun and is often good therapy for hospice patients and their families.

Medical Aspects of Laughter

Support for the healing aspects of humor is found in the Bible in the book of Proverbs 17:22—"A cheerful heart is a good medicine but a downcast spirit dries up the bones." From author Henry Ward Beecher, "Grim care, moroseness, anxiety—all this rust of life ought to be scoured off by the oil of mirth. Mirth is God's medicine." British philosopher, Bertrand Russell states, "Laughter is the most inexpensive and most effective wonder drug. Laughter is universal medicine."

With contemporary research, there is a better understanding of laughter and how it relates to human physiology. Laughter relaxes blood vessels, increases blood flow, reduces stress and anxiety and enhances mental sharpness. Further, it produces the hormone endorphin that is a natural painkiller. Brain mappings show changes in brain function that result from laughter. The neurotransmitter dopamine, the "feel good" chemical, stimulates parts of the brain associated with humor.

Recently, a Swedish research group utilized "laughter yoga" to treat cancer patients. The cancer group did deep breathing exercises followed by neck and shoulder stretches. Finally, laughter occurred when greeted with, "Ho-Ho-Ho" or "Ha-Ha-Ha." Initially, the laughter was fake but later developed into the real thing as the subjects could not stop. The laughter had a positive effect on the patients' health, both psychologically and physiologically.

Norman Cousins, former editor of the *Saturday Evening Review*, in his 1979 book, *Anatomy of an Illness,* reaffirmed the relationship of emotions to one's health status. He talked about his affliction with heart disease and a rare form of arthritis. Rather than accept the "gloom and doom" of illness that followed, he speculated if negative feelings contribute to ill health, laughter and humor should have a positive effect. He maintained a positive attitude and sought treatments, some contrary to conventional medicine.

Cousins recognized that humor could be visual. To this end, he formulated a self-directed wellness program. That included funny movies of the Marx Brothers and episodes of *Candid Camera*. The uncontrollable laughter that followed promoted relaxation, increased pain tolerance and induced sleep. Within weeks, he returned to work well on the way to recovery. Cousins suggested laughter helped him return to health.

Other anecdotal evidence from people with terminal illnesses supports Cousin's contention. In spite of his cure, the role of laughter to heal is still not well-known. However, the literature is full of references, including from the American Cancer Society, that suggest laughter reduces stress and promotes relaxation.

The Laughter Heals Foundation advocates laughter to aid in healing and provides resources and programs for laymen and the medical community. Patients' reactions to laughter programs have been favorable. To quote one person with terminal illness, "I feel healthy when I laugh." That's a strong endorsement for its use regardless of one's health condition.

Some medical centers now offer humor therapy for cancer patients and others with chronic disease. They train people to become "laughter leaders." The sessions involve joke periods, clown appearances and/or funny movies. Some programs, such as "Caring Clowns," use costumed volunteers who greet patients with a smile and/or a story to spook cancer. This approach helps establish rapport and reduces barriers between patient and staff. Patients become amused and less consumed with physical condition.

Hunter Campbell "Patch" Adams, a physician, social activist and author relies on humor and play to connect with patients that he feels are important to their physical and emotional health. His life led to the movie "Patch Adams," starring Robin Williams, who plays the doctor who does not look or act the part. For him, humor is good medicine and he will do most anything to get his patients to laugh. That includes "clowning around."

When I relate the medicinal aspects of laughter in my speeches on "Hospice and Humor," I silently transform myself into a clown with outrageous attire that includes an orange wig, red clown nose and green granny glasses. The audience, surprised by the sudden visual outburst, generally responds with laughter, or at least polite chuckles, as they don't know what to think.

Some physicians see the power of humor in themselves as a stress reducer for both doctor and patient. Dr. O.C. Simonton, a well-known cancer researcher and public speaker, suggests, "Laughter and play break up hopelessness." He agrees with Cousins that emotions influence health. Much like Patch Adams, he employs playful antics, a bit on the outrageous side, to generate laughter. He will pass marshmallows to his audiences to encourage juggling—his fascination. When frustrated with lack of success in the process, the audience thinks of other things to do with the mushy edibles. As he senses what's about to happen, Simonton puts on a football helmet and uses an umbrella for protection when bombarded with a multitude of the white objects.

Simonson's physician colleagues, Steve Allen Jr. (son of entertainers Steve Allen and Jayne Meadows) and Barry Berkowitz also share an obsession for juggling to elicit humor. Allen passes out scarves to his audience and instructs them to be creative and silly (Can you imagine juggling pieces of cloth?) and Berkowitz roves about as he juggles a hypodermic syringe, bedpan and stethoscope. The juggling doctors create humor for themselves and patients that reduces stress and promotes health.

PART 2
Humor and Conversation

CHAPTER 4

My Humor

Actress and media personality Megan Mullally suggests that a key to humor/comedy "is allowing you to look stupid." Lots of my humor makes fun of self. I am very good at that and can do so with little effort. I used to suffer embarrassment when people took notice of my flaws. However, through the years, I have learned to live with my ineptitudes and actually enjoy the humor I get from them. From writer William Arthur, "To make mistakes is human, to stumble is commonplace, and to be able to laugh at yourself is maturity."

Sometimes humor takes the form of good-natured teasing of which I get more than my share. I am an easy target. If you believe you only tease people you like,

I have a multitude of friends. I recently received a birth-day greeting from a good friend with whom I share lots of teasing. The card stated, "Life would be boring with-out the occasional goofball—Happy Birthday to one of them." I was pleased.

I am sensitive to the population with whom I use hu-mor. Hospice patients are generally older adults not only with major health issues but also with cognitive deficits related to aging. Therefore, I try to separate my fun con-fusion-based humor, which they comprehend and enjoy, from aging or disease confusion. While there is some art involved to make this distinction, it also requires an in-stinctual awareness.

As I make fun of self, patients have an opportunity to pass taunts on to me. My questions often lead to an-swers that exploit their sense of humor and encourage good-natured teasing. I once asked a feisty patient as he prepared to eat dinner if he wanted to hear a song. He grinned and quickly responded, "Give me a chance to leave first." To the same guy, I asked (knowing full well that a zinger was coming), "Do I look good?" He fol-lowed, "You should brush your teeth." He enjoyed the frivolity and so did I.

While some people might not find this type of humor funny, it is not offensive to others and is politically cor-rect. (At least, I think it is.) The use of humor is most effective when it happens spontaneously. While I think I never run out of humorous anecdotes, my wife and children frequently remind me of a tendency to repeat things. With increased age, my memory has begun to fail. I am told it's common for me to share the same stories with the same people with little time elapsing between episodes.

Once I told a patient one of my favorite stories. As I shared (what I thought to be a humorous adventure), he looked bored and gave me no more than a tepid reaction. I felt rejected and asked why he didn't like the story. He responded it wasn't quite as funny the third time around. I learned from the experience. Now, before I tell stories, I give lead-ins and inquire if the recipients heard them before. I sense my hospice patients are grateful for this gesture.

With a willingness to share my flaws for the sake of humor, here is my list. I am geographically challenged, mechanically inept and have a propensity for embarrassing experiences. I also greet everyone with a rousing "Happy Birthday," relive old "jock" stories, share humor provided by grandchildren, coin nicknames, have fun with "words," tell jokes/stories and use slapstick comedy.

Geographically Challenged

My poor sense of direction makes traveling difficult. Even after 45 years, I still have problems as I navigate in my hometown of Oshkosh, Wisconsin—not the largest of cities. In our retirement years, when my wife and I decided to spend time as "Winter Texans," our friends were amazed we could find our way to the Lone Star State without getting lost. My response to them—"Once we got to Los Angeles we were fine." In the hopes to compensate for these deficiencies, my son gave us a GPS unit. While helpful, we still encounter difficulties. No technology or gimmick is foolproof for us.

Early in my tenure at the hospice home, I came clean and confessed that I had no sense of direction. I hoped if the flaw surfaced, staff would understand and help in a crisis. They did for a while, but gradually ran out of patience. Even after six years as I roam the halls, I still have difficulty locating patients' rooms. You would think I could remember since there are only 12. As I flounder to navigate the labyrinth, observers look in disbelief and chuckle. I'm always relieved when I find the targeted room and so are the patients, particularly around lunchtime.

Mechanically Inept

Andy Rooney in his book, *Out of His Mind*, suggests, "We need more people who are handy and can do things with their hands." I so admire people who have these skills. Unfortunately, I'm not one of them. While I like to do physical work and get my hands dirty, I'm only good at things that don't require mechanical aptitude. On a 1-10 scale, I rate a minus 5. My wife is much more mechanical.

Most people are. As I trim the lawn, my frantic call for my beloved spouse signals yet another mechanical crisis. I'm out of trimming line and need a replacement cartridge, which I rely on her to attach.

My son helps the old man when in need, which is most of the time. Much like his mother, he can do most anything and is a terrific problem solver. I always have a list of "challenging" things for him to do (e.g., to start a generator for back-up electricity, to assemble anything with two or more parts, or to teach me how to use the remote control on a new TV set). To no one's surprise, he adheres to the K.I.S.S. (Keep it Simple Stupid) principle when he tutors me. If my "can do almost anything wife" is unable to accomplish the task and my son is not available, I pass the challenge to my talented neighbor. If he can't, which is a rare occurrence, he gives the job to someone else. The system works.

Unfortunately, the system only works at my home. Most patients, who have experienced my mechanical flaws, find them humorous. They think I must be joking for no one could be so inept. However, the hospice staff has been around me along enough to know the glitches are for real. Any task that requires more than a screwdriver remains a challenge. I'm afraid of failure when asked to attach wheelchair footrests, adjust beds or perform any mechanical function. Staff members no longer have the patience to assist me with the tasks, but prefer to see me fumble. Perhaps it's sadistic pleasure. However, I remain undaunted and will do anything to make people laugh at my expense. Call me a masochist.

Several months ago Sister Sue asked if I could repair a footstool. To my surprise, she was unaware of my inability to fix anything. In that I didn't want to disappoint her, I smiled and agreed to do so. The footstool is still in my garage where it gathers dust. I hope my son, in a weak moment, will restore it. Fortunately for me, Sister has yet to inquire about its status.

Propensity for Embarrassing Experiences

Based on my mechanical ineptitude and no sense of direction, it comes as no surprise that I've had more than my share of embarrassing experiences. Added to those flaws are ones that are more recent. These include memory deficits and recall deficiencies, which add to my reputation as a scatterbrain. Now in my 70s, I console myself that it happens to people as they become older. Some just have more problems than others.

Perhaps my most embarrassing experience occurred following a professional presentation at a conference in the twilight of my career. I had just finished a 2-hour lecture in front of my peers and left the auditorium to unwind. From a distance, I heard my name called and observed a woman coming in my direction. Excitedly, she greeted me with a smile and a hug. While she looked familiar, I couldn't associate a name with the face. As we engaged in small talk, my mind was still on the presentation, oblivious to the person and conversation. When I asked how things were, she replied that she still worked at an area medical center. I followed, "Do you know my friend Susie Smith who works there?" To my dismay, she responded, "I am Susie Smith." A light finally came on but it was too late. I was devastated for Susie was more than a casual acquaintance. I apologized profusely on the spot. I also gave her a call after I returned from the conference to further express remorse for the brain lock. Fortunately, Susie and I are still friends.

Occasionally, when I introduce myself to a patient, he/she will remind me I've seen them before. In response, I tell them they are important to me and not to take my forgetfulness too seriously. Then I share the story about Susie. Generally, hearty laughter occurs.

My Birthday Greeting

Every day is a special day and can be a spiritual birthday as we rejoice in a new beginning. From 2 Corinthians 5:17 "So if anyone is in Christ, he is a new creation; the old has passed away; behold the new has come." Thus, I have daily opportunities to rejoice and make a difference in the lives of the patients I serve.

I'm known to greet friends, acquaintances and even strangers with a smile and a "Happy Birthday" greeting.

The salutation is ubiquitous and goes with me everywhere. While most people greet others with a "Hello,"
"Good Morning or Afternoon." or with some other appropriate salutation, I say "Happy Birthday!" The response
is generally, "It's not my birthday." That is unless I get
lucky. I use the greeting because it is an attention-getter
and creates a happy moment.

I love to salute children with this bit of frivolity and
enjoy their reactions. I recently received a phone call
from my nephew's six-year-old twins, Anthony and Mya.
Anthony started the conversation with a big hello to Papa
Jack. I greeted him with my usual, "Happy Birthday
Anthony!" As I heard adult laughter in the background,
Anthony responded excitedly, "It really is my birthday!"
Mya chimed in it was really hers too and it truly was.

My nephew took the phone and related what led to
the call. As the kids celebrated their special day, Anthony
asked if he could call Papa Jack. When his dad asked why,
he answered that he wanted to find out if I would greet
him as I usually do. If so, he would tell me it really was
his birthday. I'm glad I didn't disappoint him. What a
great moment it was for all of us.

I find the "Happy Birthday" recipient will often try
to beat me to the punch as we cross paths. I said "Happy
Birthday" to Christian, a 12-year-old neighbor boy, a
number of times and, as expected, always got a puzzled
look. Finally, one day as I observed his confusion, I related

this was my way to greet him. Christian smiled and looked relieved. When I saw him the next day, he quickly said "Happy Birthday Mr. Kile." It was important he greet me first. To this day, we have a contest to see who's the quickest. Similarly, when I first delivered the salutation to Haley, an 11-year-old girl at church, she was expectedly confused. However, when she learned the intent, she became a player and, much like Christian, devised ways to greet me first. Her most successful strategy has been to sneak behind me and excitedly shout, "Happy Birthday!" When successful, which is most of the time, she relishes the moment and gloats in the accomplishment. These occurrences are fun and generate conversation.

I use the welcome with many hospice patients who, over time, often reciprocate. Recently, I overheard a family refer to me as the "Happy Birthday Person." While I just heard fragments of the conversation, I felt good for their smiles suggested a happy experience.

When a person reports a birthday or has just celebrated one, I give the honoree a HUMOROUS birthday card. I follow the greeting with a smile and sing a happy song. Generally, they return the smile and enjoy the vocal. The other day I greeted a patient with my standard "Happy Birthday." With a grin, he replied, "Every time I see you, I become older. I must be 100 by now, and I really feel my age!" Some people, on to my ploy, will substitute the salutation with another such as "Merry Christmas," or "Happy Anniversary." I am surprised at the interest my obsession with birthdays has on others. While reluctant to talk about the special day, they appreciate the gesture and like the attention. Sometimes when I receive cards from families of patients after their death, they end the note with a "Happy Birthday Jack!" I'm a grateful recipient.

I once presented a birthday card to Rachel, a social worker for hospice. With a puzzled look, she thanked me for the card three-months early. While the credibility of my sources took a hit, Rachel, always efficient and organized, filed the card and retrieved it on her birthday for all to see. Some people go out of their way to let me know when a birthday is about to occur, a not so subtle hint for a card. I readily comply and am amazed how grateful they are. In addition to verbal acknowledgements, I receive thank you cards and telephone calls for the small gesture of kindness. It reminds me of the song, "Little Things Mean a Lot."

While most people appear satisfied to commemorate their birthdays one day a year, others prefer to extend the festivities. My friend Betsy, with a birthday in August, prefers to celebrate the entire month with a series of gala events. While I like her style, to purchase 30 birthday cards stresses my budget and as a compromise, I give her a card a week.

I don't keep records of people's birthdays. It would be much more efficient if I did, but then there wouldn't be the element of surprise. When a person expresses

disappointment that I missed his/her special day, I apolo-
gize and send them a card. I have a favorite store that sells
them at a reasonable price. I select each card carefully to
make a personalized greeting based on personalities and
interests. Most of them have a humorous side. The selection of birthday cards is an important part of my daily
routine.

Out of curiosity, I determined how widespread my
"Happy Birthday" greeting was. Recently, I reviewed the
20 most recent emails from friends and acquaintances and
found 12 of them wished me a "Happy Birthday." Wow!
That's 60%! This little bit of fun has had more of a positive impact than I could ever imagine.

Reliving Old Jock Stories

*(I was an athlete in my day and "outstanding in my
field." To this day, I love to exchange stories about sports
to anyone that will listen. That includes a number of
hospice patients who too were athletes. We try to outdo
each other as we boast about our accomplishments. There
is a tendency to relive these experiences with a bit of hy-
perbole. "Old jocks never die, their clippings just turn
yellow." However, not all talk is about success on the
playing field. In fact, some stories establish a new standard for mediocrity. Such is the account included below.
Fortunately, for the person involved, it turns out to have
a successful conclusion. Stories, such as these, are generally funny, at least to those who have been there.)*

While some jock stories are fun to talk about, others are painful to recall. An old guy, who I know pretty well, had his athletic career get off to a good start only to have it spiral downward. He was an excellent athlete in the late 1940s and early 50s. In his pre-teen years, he made all-star little league teams in baseball and football. However, puberty came much later than his peers. At 15-years of age, his voice had not changed nor did the physique he had as a 12-year-old. However, he still loved sports, had a competitive spirit and wanted to be a team member. The mind was strong but the body weak. At five feet two inches tall and a strapping 115 pounds "soaking wet," this high school sophomore went out for football.

The check-in was memorable. Amid laughs and taunts, he waited patiently at the end of the line for football gear. When his turn came, he got leftovers—football pants with a size 42 waist, a triple "X" large jersey and an old leather football helmet, much too big for his youthful head. The gridiron attire was not a pretty sight and drew snickers from his peers.

Off to practice he went that began with a rigorous regimen of calisthenics. While under normal circumstances he could excel at jumping jacks, the task became a challenge when he couldn't keep his pants up. The girth of the leggings was not a good match for a 26-inch waist. Safety pins did not help and suspenders were not available. In a panic, he tried to catch the pants before they reached the ground without a disruption in the exercise—a challenge to say the least.

When the team scrimmaged, the excessively large helmet would slip over his eyes and darkness prevailed. The loss of vision was a blessing in disguise for he didn't see what was about to hit him. It was brutal when the big bruisers ran him over.

Everyone out for the team dressed for home games. As our friend trotted on the field, with a handgrip on the waist of his pants, he drew attention from the crowd. As he ran on the field for the first game, he lost his grip as well as his pants and drew a 15-yard penalty for indecent exposure. Admittedly, that's a bit of exaggeration, but the rest of the story is the painful truth. The year of football was a disaster.

It's been 55 years since the episode but still painful to talk about. Fortunately, this guy survived the humiliation. By his senior year, he grew 10 inches, added 50 pounds and acquired a baritone voice. He was a decent player but nothing special. Little did anyone think he would ever play football in college, but he did. He was a poster child for the late bloomer. That person is none other than the infamous "Killer" Kile.

Humor Provided by Grandchildren

Much of my interaction with hospice patients shares experiences with children and grandchildren. Often, people prefer to talk about grandchildren who are more fun. For many patients, family is their lifeline and to reminisce is important. They like to share light stories that amuse and entertain. It's a reciprocal thing for they like to hear about my family as well.

Over 50 years ago, Art Linkletter wrote a best-selling book, *Kids Say the Darndest Things.* The book is an anthology of humorous anecdotes candidly spoken by children. While I did not record these special moments with my three children, I have for my five grandchildren.

My oldest grandson Brady has always been a good source for quotes that support his precocity. As a six-year-old, his favorite place to go was the local Barnes and Noble bookstore. One day as I scanned the store's section on light humor, he was engrossed in a book on U.S. history as he memorized all the presidents' names in sequence. I saluted him for his intelligence and asked if he thought I was smart too since I was a college professor. Without hesitation, Brady looked me straight in the eye and said, "I think you're more funny than smart." That's one of my favorite quotes that I share with hospice patients.

At about the same age, a couple of other memorable incidents evoked "Bradyisms" that still bring laughter.

Once he remained in the car while his mother went to the bank. When she took longer to transact the business than he thought reasonable, he activated the car horn and waved his arms frantically. As his mother rushed to his defense, he shouted, "I was afraid you were about to become victimized!"

In another instance, I observed a used farm tractor on the lot of a local farm implement store that looked familiar. When I asked Brady about it, he reported it had been a tractor from the family farm. As a follow-up, I inquired if it had been a serviceable machine, Brady replied, "No! It's a piece of junk, but some sucker will probably buy it." I wonder if he had heard that from someone else.

Eighteen years have passed and Brady is a college graduate. He earned a B.A degree (magnum cum laude) with a major in chemistry. The content of his senior thesis "Synthesis and Electrochemical Behavior of a Functionalized {2} Catenane and Electrochemical Behavior of Benzylic Amide {2} Catenane," stirred up deep intellectual discussions between him and me (I lie a lot; I can't even pronounce the title.) He just earned a Master's Degree in Organic Chemistry from a Big Ten University. His "more funny than smart" grandfather is very proud.

Brady's sisters, Kesley and Ashley, haven't provided as many humorous quotes as their older brother, but they are terrific kids who are fun, bright and successful.

Kesley, who just completed her junior year in college, has always been very close to her mother (my daughter). At age three, she was the flower girl in her aunt's wedding. Her task at the event was to march down the aisle hand-in-hand with a little boy who was the ring bearer. Out of fright, she refused and the ring bearer entered by himself. As her mother (the matron of honor) appeared, there was a frightened little girl with her arms wrapped around her mother's legs. It made for a difficult walk to the altar for the twosome and truly was a Kodak moment.

Ashley, who just graduated from high school, has always had a love for animals. She grew up on a dairy farm and has always had a special attachment to the cows. Her all-time favorite was a heifer named Clever. As a six-year-old, Ashley saw Clever daily. When she entered the barn, the heifer would rush to greet her. There was a special connection between the two. As a remembrance, Ashley still has Clever's ear tag displayed on the rear view mirror of her car.

Ashley also had a fondness and compassion for calves. When they had their horns removed, she would comfort them as they recovered from the trauma. Once she told me, "Papa, I love animals. When I grow up, I want to be a "vegetarian." About the same time, she asked her parents for horse riding lessons. When they said she was too young, with disgust, she replied, "I hate my body."

My younger grandson Jack (a cousin of Brady, Kesley and Ashley) has also had a share of special moments. Once I tried to console him when ill. As I stroked his head, I asked the three-year-old if he still had a fever. Without hesitation, Jack responded, "I don't have a fever Papa, I just feel hot because I'm warm-blooded." When I told him he was a beautiful child, he said, "I'm not beautiful papa, I'm handsome." Once when irritated as I teased him, Jack lectured, "I don't trust you anymore, and once you lose trust, it's hard to get back."

Now tops in his fourth grade class, Jack does not lack in self-confidence. Recently, as a classroom activity, the kids were supposed to come up with words ending in "tion." While most of his classmates selected words like "nation," "motion," or "lotion," he blurted out "arbitration." Coincidently, both of his parents are attorneys. In another incident, Jack's mother praised him for his efforts on a standardized achievement test in which he a scored 99%. While most would be ecstatic over the accomplishment, with a look of disappointment, he asked, "What did I get wrong?"

While a super star in the classroom, Jack hasn't yet excelled in sports, but he doesn't know that. Once when playing goalie on his soccer team, he seldom moved or attempted to block the shots. As ball-after-ball flew by for scores, he waved his arms in disgust and shouted, "I can't do it all by myself!"

Even as a preschooler, Grace (Jack's sister and our youngest grandchild) was a "social butterfly," and a great conversationalist. When I asked her whether she was a boy or girl, she quickly responded, "I'm a princess Papa." When I inquired if she was a baby, her retort was "I'm not a baby, I'm a toddler." When Grace tried to explain discomfort from a sore throat, she said, "I have a swallow ache."

Another memorable incident occurred shortly after her parents went to a masquerade party that left quite an impression. My son Todd found Grace in her room with the lights on as she sat on the edge of the bed. When he asked why she wasn't sleeping, she replied, "I'm afraid of monsters." When told not to be afraid of monsters for she could always talk to Jesus and ask for help, she thought about it for a few minutes and went back to bed. About 15-minutes later, she came downstairs with a look of bewilderment. When asked, what was wrong, Grace replied, "Jesus can't talk because he's just a baby." The incident occurred in January and the Christmas story was still fresh in her mind.

Once when Grace painted make-up on the carpet, her parents didn't feel she deserved a treat. Shortly thereafter, she said, "I don't feel good." When asked what the matter was, she responded, "I have a sickness called NOT FAIR." In another instance, when I tried to initiate a conversation, she did not want any distractions as she watched a favorite television show and tersely said, "Talk to somebody else."

She had her priorities that did not include Papa. Stories about Grace abound when patients and I share fun stories about grandchildren.

Nicknames

I've always been a big proponent of nicknames. They're generally used with people you like and signify friendship. Some have interesting histories and some don't. In any case they're fun. I love to give out nicknames to family and friends. Many occur for no apparent rhyme or reason. I call my grandson Jack—"Johnny Appleseed," my daughter Toni—"Billy Jo," and my son Todd—"Rodney." Recently, a woman expressed warm memories about her grandfather who was a hospice patient. In the conversation, she mentioned the nickname he gave her—"Scary Sara the Siberian Soup Sipper." That's quite a mouthful for a person named Janet. She didn't know what precipitated the tomfoolery from grandpa but she enjoyed every minute of it.

Some nicknames make sense for they're similar to the real thing. I call my other grandson "Bradley" whose name is Brady and my granddaughter "Kesey," whose name is Kesley and Kesley's sister Ashley "A.J.," the initials of her first and last names. Our youngest granddaughter Grace's self-proclaimed nickname is "Daphne," her favorite Scooby-Doo character. Finally, my daughter

Tammy's nickname is "Whamo," from when she played softball.

I frequently greet people unintentionally with the incorrect name. When the faux pas occurs several times (sometimes on purpose), I conveniently convert the mistaken name to the nickname. That is if the designee doesn't have a problem with it. Barb, a staff nurse, has adjusted to the name Gladys and now calls me George. That exchange often brings weird looks and whispered comments from those listening to the conversation.

The other day, I mistakenly called Jane, a patient, "Betty." When she corrected me, I remained calm and indicated that while I have a good memory, it's short. Further, I told her it was an easy mistake to make for Betty and Jane sound similar. Now she doesn't know what to think.

Occasionally, I will fabricate outrageous names to introduce myself. One patient, who I had met before, recognized me, but couldn't remember my name. When I introduced myself as Felix Farquart from the Farquart Pickle Factory, he smiled and went along with the gag. The next week he greeted me with a smile and said "Hi Felix! Where are my pickles?" I remained Felix to him.

I love my nickname "Killer" and its connotation that I'm a tough guy. It has a long illustrious history that goes back to my college football days. As a fierce cornerback, I once blocked a pass inadvertently with my nose. As I ran off the field, blood gushed from my nostrils, and I was a sorry sight. In disgust, I took the palm of my hand and wiped the blood on my white jersey, which rapidly took on a scarlet color. It got my coach's attention and with a grin he said, "You look like a "Killer." The name stuck and today I am "Killer" to many.

When I meet male patients with an interest in sports, I often announce my nickname and give a brief history of the moniker. I then flash the fierce "Killer" football stance and wait for reactions. Usually there is laughter that sets a good foundation for an exchange of humor. Perhaps the most memorable experience with my nickname came when I visited a patient and quickly discovered there were two "Killers."

The "Killer" nickname generally sticks with people and is easier to remember than "Jack." However, every now and then a substitute nickname appears that has a similar meaning. One patient, who recognized my would-be tough guy image, would snicker and greet me with, "Hello Animal!" After he utilized the salutation several weeks in succession (being corrected each time), he relented one day and with a huge grin said, "You're Killer!" I think he knew the whole time. He had fun with the nickname.

Sometimes the nickname catches on with others. At a funeral of one of my hospice patients, the son of the deceased introduced me to other family members as "Killer," one of his dad's good friends. That was good to hear for his father and I had connected through humor and had fun together.

Fun with Words

I've always had an interest in words and still seek meanings from my trusted dictionary, a high school graduation present. While tattered and torn, the book, with highlighted words, serves as a subtle reminder of my vocabulary growth. With some patients, I throw out "64 dollar" words to create a fun experience. For example, "I don't want to appear **pedantic** for fear of being a **dilettante**." "I also tend to be **ostentatious** and **pretentious** but never **redundant**." Those that understand the vernacular are often amused while others are confused. However, most seem to appreciate the frivolity.

One of my classic greetings, once I've established rapport, is "It's a **severe** pleasure to see you." While many, at least initially, don't understand the significance of **severe** (nor do I), they sense it's a fun way to say "Hello" that's just a little unconventional. After several visits, some patients, eager to participate in the frivolity, return the greeting.

I enjoy the use of adult words with small children to get reactions. I asked my youngest granddaughter at three years of age if she were **precocious**. She responded, "No Papa—I'm Gracie." A year later, I asked her again. This time she recognized her precocity and responded, "Yes—I'm smart." Admittedly, her parents tutored along the way, but I was still impressed.

I intentionally misuse words that sound similar (malapropisms). Norm Crosby, the master of this confusion, speaks from the **diaphragm** and likes **decapitated** coffee. I enjoy the use of malapropisms with some hospice patients. There is a range of reactions to the nonsense. Most recipients find amusement in the dialogue, while others do not catch the errors or find humor in them. Some people perceive the mistakes as the result of my ignorance and correct me. When these instances occur, I smile and thank them.

Here is a list of my favorites:

*"I make mistakes. I'm not **inflammable**."
*"I don't have to take those false **incinerations**."
*"Please stop. You're **irrigating** me."
*"I'm equally adept at using each hand. I am **amphibious**."
*"I **resemble** that remark."
*"You look really **extinguished** in that outfit."
*"While Spanish was her native language, she was also **fluid** in English."
*"On this **hysterical** occasion, let's reflect on what's happened in the past."

*"The barbershop chorus will **conjugate** backstage to get ready for the show."

*"I have a tough time making decisions and have a tendency to **prognosticate**."

*"The discussion on the topic was not pertinent and totally **irreverent**."

Sometimes an unintentional faux pas occurs. One hospice patient of German heritage, when he returned from travels in the southeastern United States reported, "Those **Application Mountains** are really something." From another, "I have had so many chemotherapy and **radar** treatments, I can't remember."

Slapstick Comedy

I love to tell jokes and stories and receive personal satisfaction when people laugh. I'm not always certain whether the laughter is the result of funny material or intended for me. The reason is not important.

Performances by my barbershop quartets create a wonderful forum for laughter. We like to amuse audiences with fun songs and parodies and to tell a story or two. The key to elicit laughter is in the delivery and timing. Some people are natural storytellers, and with a few embellishments, are able to tickle one's "funny bone." Now that I'm older, I often focus on geriatric humor.

(Henry and Estelle, married for over 60 years, disagreed about most things and could not live with or without each other. Estelle liked to talk and Henry did not like to listen (at least to her). She thought she was in charge and Henry wanted her to think she was. One day Estelle craved a chocolate ice cream sundae and requested he get her one. As she told him what she wanted for toppings, fearful that he would forget, she asked that he write them down. He assured her he would remember and rushed off to do the errand. About an hour later, he returned, not with a chocolate sundae, but with a cheese sandwich. Estelle was furious he didn't get what she requested. When asked what he forgot, Estelle quickly replied, "You forgot the mustard.")

Once when I told this story to a hospice patient, he looked me straight in the eye and asked, "What's so funny?" As he observed my look of shock, he broke out into laughter. I felt relieved.

I love slapstick comedy. Give me such comedic icons as W.C. Fields, Laurel and Hardy or Martin and Lewis and I laugh right on key. However, my all time favorite is the Bud Abbot and Lou Costello "Who's on First" routine. One of my prized possessions, a gift from my children, is an animated figurine of Bud and Lou all decked out in their baseball attire. With the press of a button, the skit comes to life for all to hear. Sometimes I take the statuette with me on hospice visits.

I am also happy to share my collection of DVDs of classic comedy shows with patients. In addition to comediennes mentioned above, patients can laugh and reminisce to such legends as "Lucy," "Dick Van Dyke," "Ozzie and Harriet," "Andy Griffith," "The Little Rascals," and "Popeye." Sometimes family and staff (on their break of course) join the patient in watching the videos. It's great therapy for everyone.

CHAPTER 5

My Fun Conversations with Hospice Patients

I enjoy my weekly visits with hospice patients and try to initiate conversations that focus attention on them. When volunteer and patient have common interests, conversation thrives and visits are productive. I continue to be amazed how quickly relationships develop, and how open these people are to share feelings and emotions. Unless patients want to discuss their illness and health issues, I focus on positive things. During conversation, I try to be a COMPASSIONATE LISTENER and maintain eye contact to show interest and recognize that silence (a real challenge for me) sometimes stimulates conversation. Further as suggested by Leo Buscaglia, author of *Learning and Loving*, I am reminded I can best serve these people if I don't impose myself or value systems on them.

Once I establish rapport with hospice patients, a door often opens and communication flows. These people share happy moments and humorous experiences as well as cathartic incidents related to illness. Although merry times are fleeting, they give patients a respite from their illnesses that consume them. At the same time, reflective moments occur that are heart-rending and bring out the best in people. Often, experiences are spiritual and reflect a strong faith and anticipation of another life to come.

To generate conversations with patients, generally in their senior years, I seek light topics to establish rapport and promote enjoyment and am reluctant to bring up controversial subjects (e.g., politics, the economy). Talk about family (with an emphasis on children and grandchildren) often brings joy and contentment. Living in Wisconsin, Packer football is a hot topic for everyone. Men like to talk about adventures when they fish and hunt. They also enjoy humorous stories, and to hear about my ineptitudes. Women frequently share entertainment experiences such as their favorite television shows and trips to the casinos. Food is a popular topic and they like to share their favorite recipes and food preparation. Music communicates with all. Big band music is a favorite as is polka music. Patients generally enjoy the old songs (even with me doing the singing).

My use of humor is generally spontaneous and takes place without a plan. I initiate it when appropriate and view it as a major instrument to give patients emotional and spiritual support. When I establish an environment conducive to humor, some patients will beat me to the punch and initiate the frivolity. Once when I greeted a patient, he began the conversation and told me to consider a product that was on sale at a local store. With a straight face he said, "Buy one, pay for two and get the second one free." As I quickly exited his room supposedly to shop for the item, there was laughter. It made my day.

PART 3
Hospice and Music

CHAPTER 6

Smiling with Music and Song

Jonathan Edwards, a noted singer/songwriter, states "The best, most beautiful and most perfect way that we have of expressing sweet concord of mind to each other is by music." The use of music is a component in hospice palliative care programs. The comfort it provides the sick has had a long and illustrious history that dates back to Aristotle and Plato. The approach to music varies with the interests and health condition of the patient. While still alert, it can create happy moods and thoughts for the patient and provide comfort and support for the family as their loved one nears death.

The "Golden Oldies"

As a real ham, I like to sing to hospice patients, at least to those that have sympathetic ears. I have no musical background and do not read music. Thanks to my mother, who was an excellent alto singer, I do have an ear for harmony (at least some say I do) and love to sing the old songs. For the past 40 years, I have sung in barbershop quartets. I am in my element when I sing such standards as "My Wild Irish Rose," "Down by the Old Mill Stream," or "For Me and My Gal." When younger, my kids were always amused that this was my kind of music, and old dad wasn't very cool. Now as adults (all in their 40s), they find it semi-tolerable. The music creates nostalgia and is a great way to connect with people in their senior years. I use it generously with hospice patients.

My signature song is "When You're Smiling." Mark Fisher, Joe Goodwin & Larry Shey composed the song in 1928 (a year after Babe Ruth hit 60 home runs). Louie "Satchmo" Armstrong put the words to the music. The lyrics suggest a smile is a reciprocal thing. Have you ever noticed when you approach someone with a smile, the person returns the pleasantry and conversation thrives?

Music has the power to churn up all sorts of emotions. People can feel down and out only to snap out of the funk when they hear a cheery song. Such is the case with

"Powder Your Face with Sunshine," a song written by Carmen Lombardo and Stanley Rochinski in 1948. The lyrics suggest smiles lead to laughter; they cure the blues and brighten the future.

To sing the "golden oldies" can create happy moods and resurrect fond memories. Often patients will sing along or mouth familiar lyrics and will laugh when parodies occur. As a barbershopper, I have lots of them.

Something special occurs when you sing a cappella in harmony (ask any barbershopper) and I never miss an opportunity to do so. Sometimes, a patient joins in the songfest, as do family and friends, and harmonious chords ring throughout the room. My barbershop quartet frequently takes its show on the road to sing for shut-ins (e.g., private homes, hospice homes, nursing homes, hospitals).

Big Band and Polka Music

A number of hospice patients grew up in the big band era to the beat of such icons as the Dorsey Brothers, Benny Goodman and Harry James. My in-laws loved big band music and were excellent ballroom dancers in their day. Even in their 80s, they never missed an opportunity to dance to the lively music. When their dancing days were over, they would still listen to the classics and tap their feet to the rhythm. I'm always fascinated when patients passionately share their experiences from the big band era. As they reminisce and listen to the music, health, for a moment, is not an issue and happy thoughts reflect what used to be.

Many refer to Wisconsin as the polka capitol of the world. Such polka legends as Frankie Yankovic still conjure up excitement and seniors still passionately strut on the dance floor at fests and social events. For some patients, their dancing to this unique style of music is only a recent memory. They love to reminisce and are receptive listeners when they hear such favorites as "Just Because," and "Beer Barrel Polka."

Hymns and Gospel Music

Many patients have strong beliefs and music can result in a religious experience. To sing hymns and spiritual numbers, such as "How Great Thou Art," and "Amazing Grace," often give them peace and contentment.

I'm a big fan of gospel music, particularly the southern gospel type, which features quartet and choral vocals with a strong emphasis on harmony. The high energy level and spirituality of these groups are inspirational. Through the efforts of Bill Gaither (a gospel singer and songwriter), there has been a revival of southern gospel music and his Homecoming concerts have played throughout the world. I have a collection of Gaither's CDs and DVDs that I share with patients.

Soothing Music

Sometimes soft music soothes the patient in the latter stages of illness. It might be recorded or live. Therese Schroeder-Sheker developed "Music Thanatology" (derived from the Greek word for death) which involves live harp music for use with people near death.

Rebecca, a talented harpist/singer, comes to the Home every week to play for patients and families. The music creates peacefulness and tranquility that often puts the patient in a contented state and gives the family support. This helps create an inner peace and preparation for death. Some patients plan their funerals that include this special music.

PART 4
Patient Stories Involving Humorous and Heart-Rending Experiences

This segment of the book, for the most part, includes sketches of patients I have served at the hospice home but also includes a few in other settings (e.g., patients' homes, nursing homes, assisted living centers, hospitals). I knew a few of the people before illness, some as close friends and others as acquaintances.

The 59 vignettes, often interspersed with humor and song, consist of isolated stories as well as heart-rending experiences incorporated into biographical sketches, some with more detail than others. Some are included with quotes when available. All but five relate to my experiences with hospice patients. These stories are true, to my best recollection. I have avoided the use of real names to respect confidentiality.

In the sketches "Bart and Bill's Humor," and "Ted's Last Hunt," a pastor friend shares human-interest stories about his friends with terminal illness. In "Darla's Special Hug," a volunteer relates the power of the action. Finally, in "Chet's Amazing Grace," and "A Special Goodbye from Alice," two volunteers, describe their heart-rending experiences with patients. Also, there is a series of isolated stories about hospice patients that reveal unexpected humor.

I have divided this part of the book into four chapters: Chapter 7: "Stories about Patients I Saw as a Hospice Volunteer, Chapter 8: "Stories about My Friends with Terminal Illness," Chapter 9: "Stories about Patients from Friends and Hospice Volunteers," and Chapter 10: "Humorous Incidents with Patients that Involve Family, Hospice Staff and Volunteers."

CHAPTER 7

Stories about Patients I Saw as a Hospice Volunteer

"Edna and the Oppositional Wheelchair"

(Much of my humor involves poking fun of self. In this sketch, my mechanical ineptitude reared its ugly head and resulted in a humorous moment with a patient (later shared with her husband) that involved the adjustment of footrests on a wheelchair. Unfortunately, no one was available to assist me with the task. Based on this experience, I started to develop a compensatory strategy. However, I did not complete the task, for to have a system that atoned for my flaws would likely lessen the fun and humor with patients.)

Edna was a dear lady who had ALS. She possessed a marvelous attitude, indefatigable spirit and terrific sense of humor that she never lost. In her latter days, she refused to be bedridden, was always dressed and sat in her favorite lounge chair. Although no longer able to vocalize, she did her best to communicate as she mouthed words and wrote notes. Importantly, through it all, Edna never lost her delightful smile. She remained as active as she could be and loved to go for rides through the beautiful gardens that surrounded the Home.

During Edna's first few weeks as a hospice patient, her devoted husband Jim was at her side 24/7 and lovingly cared for her. Among other things, he took her for daily walks, read to her and fed her. After a while, I sensed he needed some respite and subsequently volunteered to do the special things for Edna during my weekly visit. While Jim trusted me, he still felt guilty and took the time-off with some reluctance. However, he quickly adapted and ended a leave of absence in a weekly dart ball league where his competitive spirit quickly returned. The diversion was therapeutic and his time with Edna became more special.

Fortunately, Jim wasn't around when I attempted to take Edna for her first walk. With a lack of confidence, I struggled to put the footrests on the wheelchair. The footrest identified for the left side seemed like it should be on the right side. While I fumbled to accomplish the task, Edna, who waited patiently, grinned from ear-to-ear. This was a moment for laughter. Had Edna been able to vo-calize, I can only imagine what her laughter would have sounded like.

Out of desperation, I consulted with Betsy in house-keeping for help. However, she questioned why I did not learn the task when in volunteer training. This brought another smile from Edna. After what seemed to be an eter-nity, we got the footrests aligned and took a walk. While we strolled around the grounds, Edna smiled throughout as she reflected on what had just transpired. This inci-dent provided a therapeutic outlet for Edna and the start of a wonderful friendship. When Edna and I returned, I pleaded with the staff to leave the footrests on for the sake of expediting future walks.

The wheelchair incident is one of my favorite stories when I speak to groups about my hospice experiences. To create a real life happening, I select people from the audi-ence to role-play the event. It's a humorous moment at my expense but, to make a point, I'm glad to be the giver. It goes like this.

JACK – "Edna, would you like to go for a walk? It's a beautiful day outside."

EDNA – "That would be nice."

JACK – (Goes to her wheelchair and observes the footrests are not attached.) "Wait just a minute while

I try to attach the footrests to your wheelchair. I must admit Edna that I'm not very mechanically inclined. In fact, on a 1-5 scale, I'm probably a minus 5." (Jack fumbles around for a few minutes without having any success.) "I'm really embarrassed Edna but I can't figure out how to attach the footrests. I'll ask Betsy in housekeeping for help. (Edna smiles enjoying Jack's ineptitude.)

BETSY – "What do you want Jack? You mean I have to help you again! You should know better than to try anything mechanical."

JACK – "I can't figure out how to attach the footrests to Edna's wheelchair. Can you help me?"

BETSY – "You're not very handy are you. Wow! I thought you'd be trained better to do these things."

JACK – "Stop being so critical of me and just try to help." (They inspect the footrests.) "This footrest is marked left but it seems like it should be on the right side. What do you think?"

BETSY – "Don't be silly why would it be marked left if it isn't left? Give me the footrest. I think it might go like this."

JACK – "No—That won't work. Edna's feet will never reach the footrest. She'll pull a muscle. Let's try the footrest on the other side. Do you suppose we need a screwdriver?"

BETSY – "I don't think so. I've seen staff put the footrests on in just a few seconds without any tools. I can't believe you don't know how to do it. I'm in housekeeping and this is not part of my job description to help people like you." (Through all of this, Edna continues to smile and enjoys the frivolity.)

JACK – "Come on Betsy give me a break. You want Edna to take a ride don't you?

BETSY – "All right—Let's try again. I think I got it. These nubbins go above the frame into these little holes. There we go."

JACK – "But isn't that footrest on the wrong side. It is turning out not in. I don't think Edna's foot will reach that far."

BETSY – "Okay—Let's try it the other way."

JACK – "By Jove—I believe you've got it."

BETSY – "Do me a favor Jack and write down what we did to attach the footrests so this won't happen again."

JACK – "Why would I want to do that? It wouldn't make any sense to me anyhow. Let's go for a ride Edna." (She was ready.)

Hospice volunteers often develop friendships with family members of the deceased. Since Edna's passing three years ago, Jim and I get together for lunch at least once a month. There is never a dull moment when we're together and we share in lots of laughs. When his Edna's name is mentioned, it's about happy thoughts and warm memories which includes the infamous wheelchair incident.

"Singing and Dining with Sweet Margaret"

Margaret was another one of my early patients who left a lasting impression. While unable to speak because of a brain tumor, the glow in her eyes and expression on her face let one know she understood. She had a tender, captivating smile that filled the room with positive vibes.

As one might expect, Margaret's family adored her. She was a special mother and grandmother for whom they did special things. A granddaughter frequently styled her hair and gave her manicures. Her room generally included bouquets of fragrant flowers and an array of family pictures and greeting cards, all testaments to this dear lady.

Margaret so enjoyed the daily visits from her devoted son Mike whose terrific sense of humor picked up her spirits. Mike and I became good friends. It didn't take long for him to identify my flaws and fun teasing ensued. One day as he observed my difficulty to adjust his mother's bed (too much of a challenge for my mechanical skills), he completed the task with ease and chuckled as he did so. I felt humiliated and stated, "I make mistakes; I'm not **inflammable**." Further "I don't have to take your false **incinerations**." We had fun. Most importantly, Mike knew how much I cared about his mother.

Margaret was the first patient that I serenaded. As I prepared to sing, with a bit of uneasiness, I extended my hand. When she quickly grasped mine, apprehensions quickly subsided, and there was an immediate connection. As I began to sing, "When You're Smiling," she tightened her grip and tears rolled down her cheeks. As I continued the song, she mouthed the words and occasionally produced sound. Margaret's reaction was the litmus test that provided incentive to sing to other patients. I quickly referred to my book of lyrics that featured many of the "oldies" and initiated the first of many songfests.

Rebecca and I would sometimes visit Margaret together. Margaret so enjoyed the exquisite music on the harp provided by Rebecca and so did I. Periodically, Rebecca and I (upon my insistence) did vocal duets. Margaret became very excited when we did songs in harmony, especially "Aura Lee." I later learned that Margaret had sung with a "Sweet Adeline" group (the female equivalent to male barbershop choruses) and loved to harmonize in a cappella style.

During Margaret's 3-month stay at the Home, there was seldom a week that I didn't see her. I generally fed her lunch. She had a voracious appetite and consumed massive portions of culinary delights from the kitchen. When I entered Margaret's room with the food tray that featured a veritable buffet, she smiled from ear-to-ear. While the excitement was likely due to the food and not my appearance, it was good to see her happy.

Margaret truly enjoyed her meals, highlights of her day, and I felt privileged to feed her. I took the task seriously and made it as pleasurable as possible. In preparation for the event, with Mike's help when available, I'd adjust the bed and the slide table so she was in the optimal position to dine. I gave her plenty of time to eat. Fortunately, unlike a number of patients, Margaret was able to chew and swallow with little difficulty. In a display of my obsessive behavior, I had a separate utensil for each food type, a washcloth that I used as needed and a bib (clothing protector to be politically correct), which I changed when spillage occurred.

As I fed Margaret, we listened to some "Sweet Adeline" classics. Between bites, she would hum along as she enjoyed the best of both worlds—music and food. When finished with lunch, we would sing some "oldies" such as "My Wild Irish Rose," "Toot, Toot, Tootsie Goodbye," and "You Tell Me Your Dream," until she fell asleep contented and happy. We completed this ritual week-after-week.

I attended Margaret's funeral. As I scanned pictures that highlighted her life, there was a photo of her "Sweet Adeline" singing group. With my eyes glued on the lady in the front row with that signature smile, I imagined a beautiful alto voice as she sang, "When You're Smiling," in perfect harmony. I left with a song in my heart and many wonderful memories of a special person.

"Betty Burgers"

When I first met Betty, she greeted me with a smile and we had an instant connection. She liked to hear the old songs and I looked forward to our visits. She expected top priority treatment and requested I see her first thing in the morning. When I missed a visit, she was not a "happy camper" and demanded an explanation. There was no doubt she was in charge. However, I didn't mind for I loved her feisty spirit.

When we visited, Betty dominated the conversation and had an opinion on most subjects. Food was her favorite. She was an excellent cook and described her favorite dishes prepared from produce provided on the family farm. Her soul mate Frank, a person of few words, was usually by her side. The couple, married for over half a century, supported the adage "unlike personalities attract." They shared experiences of life on the farm where they raised prize-winning beef cattle. They set the standard high, and enjoyed the taste of premium meat.

Once when I visited Betty, I asked how her appetite was. She replied nothing tasted good. I asked if she was hungry for something. She said she longed for a hamburger, as did Frank, not from the Home's kitchen (which drew raves from most) but rather from Joe's Burger Joint, which reportedly served beef from their farm. To keep with the true spirit of hospice, I complied with their request and went to Joe's to get the burgers. Since there was no budget for special orders, I paid out of pocket and delivered the delicacies that they consumed without a word—a first for Betty.

The next week, I visited again around lunchtime (not so smart on my part). Betty reported how much she enjoyed last week's burger (as did Frank) and that they had another request. Reluctantly, I asked what it was. It was another sandwich (this time chicken) again not from the kitchen (much to the dismay of the cook), but from Joe's. I wondered if the chicken from Joe's was also from their farm but didn't have the courage to ask. Again, I filled the request much to their delight.

As I finally learned from these episodes that my timing was less than optimal, I made subsequent visits later in the afternoon. However, since the special food experience made Betty and Frank happy, I occasionally appeared at lunchtime when I had a couple of extra bucks. It was worth the expense.

"Rejection by Harriet"

(*For those hospice patients still mentally alert and with good cognitive function, there is an opportunity to form connections and look at the light side of life. Some visits do not yield positive results and rapport is difficult, at least initially. One can understand why these people are cantankerous and ill-natured. However, a sustained effort to show that you care, even in subtle ways (e.g., a pleasant hello, smile, a stroke of the hand), might change attitudes over time. Such was the case with Harriet.*)

Shortly before I met Harriet, I had a nice talk with her daughter. She spoke fondly about her mother and how she liked to play card games, particularly cribbage. As a novice player, I thought a match with Harriet might provide a good icebreaker. Further, my ineptitude at the game might feed her ego.

When I greeted Harriet, she glared and asked what precipitated the visit. I told her I was a volunteer who stopped by to say hello. When asked if that was okay, she replied tersely, "What choice do I have?" Her response only set me back a little bit for I thought my "ace in the hole" would be a fun game of cribbage. When I popped the question, she replied indignantly, "I don't want to play." That really burst my bubble and her daughter's credibility took a hit. While Harriet caught me off-guard, I smiled, wished her a good day and quietly left the room.

I had a week to regain my composure and made a return visit armed with my best smile and charm. To my surprise, she was mildly receptive to the call. As I held her hand and sang "When You're Smiling," I observed a glimpse of a smile. In view of the newfound rapport, I thought the time would be perfect for a game of cribbage. However, when asked if she wanted to play, she abruptly said, "No!" My insecurities surfaced. What had I done to deserve rejection?

In spite of Harriet's rebuff, I put her on my list to visit regularly. In the weeks that followed, Harriet began to enjoy my visits and would smile when I entered her room. However, she never accepted the offer to play cribbage. Word has it she learned of my ineptitude for the game and didn't want to play someone with inferior talent. I accepted that.

"Sam and "Killer" Kowalski"

(When patients are not active participants in conversations, do not assume they are confused and give them opportunities to respond. When Sam's auditory processing deficits were addressed, active conversation occurred.)

Sam had an inoperable brain tumor that resulted in communication problems. While he comprehended conversation, there were delays in responses as it took time for him to retrieve words. To help us communicate, I spoke slowly, used short segments and gave him time to process what he heard. While Sam searched for words, I remained silent, maintained eye contact to show interest and patience, and took special care not to interrupt his train of thought. When responses occurred, they were appropriate and clearly stated.

Sam and I connected through our mutual interest in sports. He was quite a baseball player in his day and was a member of an American Legion team that won a state championship. Not to be out done, I boasted of my athletic prowess on the gridiron. During our visits, we shared sports stories. He laughed when I told him I was "A legend in my own mind."

When I told Sam, my football nickname was "Killer," he smiled and gave his seal of approval. I began and ended visits with my old football stance accompanied by the fierce "Killer" look. As he looked in amazement, his eyes widened and with a grin shouted, "Killer," and then provided the last name of "Kowalski!" (a professional wrestler in the early era). I thought—what a compliment to be included in that company.

I later learned that "Killer" Kowalski seldom won a match and was always the fall guy for the superstars like the Crusher or Andre the Giant. While Kowalski was famous for various moves, which included a stomach vice grip called the "Killer Clutch," he was unable to deliver the knockout punch. I think Sam tried to tell me something.

At Sam's funeral, I looked at photographs on a picture board that highlighted his life. Appropriately, they included a picture of his state championship American Legion baseball team—a lasting memory.

"Maude's Selective Memory"

Maude, a delightful lady, was in her late 90s. We developed a special relationship through a mutual interest in singing. She outlived her hospice placement and moved to a nursing home. To everyone's amazement, her condition did not change significantly over the next two years.

Maude presented the paradox of memory problems that haunt many older adults and frequently asked where she lived. I once responded—"Wisconsin." However, she wasn't looking for the state (which she knew well) but rather her residence. With a grin, she replied, "You're as far off as I am." She had me pegged. Maude could remember in detail events from childhood when she worked in her father's hardware store, raised acres of potatoes, looked for 4-leaf clovers, made sauerkraut and rode her bike throughout the countryside, but could not remember what she did a few minutes ago.

While Maude had short-term memory difficulties, she still possessed considerable intellect and a delightful wit. She had a wonderful sense of humor and loved to tease. I once asked if she thought I was good looking. She answered, "Maybe I'd better look again." While I still looked for the elusive compliment, I followed with, "Do you think I am a talented singer?" Maude quickly responded unequivocally, "Not really." At that point, I changed the tone of the conversation. Reality had set in. In another instance, I told Maude how special she was. To reciprocate, she searched for something nice to say about me, a formidable task at best. After some thought and deliberation, she responded to the challenge and stated I was also special in a <u>certain</u> way. Maude's daughter related the humorous side of her mother just recently surfaced. In the past, Maude was very prim and proper and not prone to tomfoolery or wisecracks. This change of personality at this stage of her life pleased the family.

For many years, Maude displayed her beautiful alto voice in the church choir. She loved to sing and had a good ear for harmony. While her voice had lost some of its glitter, she knew the thrill of singing well and cherished the brief moments when melodious sound returned. Maude and I often greeted each other with song. For example, I would make up a little ditty and sing, "Hello Maude— How are you today?" With a few embellishments, she would follow with an improvised tune of, "I'm fine Jackie." It was a fun way to begin a visit.

Maude had a love for the "golden oldies," which we sang together. As she became more familiar with the lyrics, I would sing a line and have her fill in a word or two. Over time, Maude memorized a number of lyrics and learned to sing some songs without assistance. Once when I complimented her for remembering the words of her favorite song, "When You're Smiling," she responded, "They were sticking back there and looking at you kind of brought them out."

Maude loved to do novelty songs and enjoyed the humor that followed. One number she enjoyed performing was "When it's Lamp Lighting Time in the Valley." (Sung to the tune "Red River Valley"). The lyrics are "When it's lamp lighting time in the valley; when it's lamp lighting time in the valley; when it's lamp lighting time in the valley; then it's lamp lighting time in the valley." Once when the repetition became obvious to her, she smiled and with a look of bewilderment asked, "Are you stuck?" We both laughed and continued the song.

One of the classics, relished by her family and friends, was a novelty tune we did together. I sang "One beer for one." She responded, "Two beers for two, I sang "Three beers for three." She followed, "AND A BARREL FOR ME." When her family heard this gem for the first time, they had a good laugh. What a great team we made.

Maude was the star and I was the fan. With such success, I suggested we should capitalize on her talents and charge for the impromptu concerts or at least pass around the hat. She was not certain turning professional was the thing to do, but would think it over.

Maude often did not recognize people she knew well, but she always remembered me and recalled the day of the week that I visited. Last year, I missed eight weeks of hospice work while on winter vacation. When I returned, the staff bet me Maude would not know who I was. I accepted the bet without reservation. A sizeable entourage accompanied me to her room to witness her reaction. As I entered, I shouted with joy, "Hi Maude—It's great to see you again!" She gazed at me in surprise and with the biggest smile ever said, "Well, for heaven sakes, if it isn't Jackie boy!" I collected on the bet.

(Footnote: One of the features of volunteer work is to have the freedom to do other things. Generally, hospice personnel are happy to have you when available. My wife and I go to a warmer climate for a couple of months in the winter and take an occasional out-of-state trip in the summer. I still feel guilty when I leave and sometimes suffer the consequences. Recently, when I returned from vacation, my attention turned to hospice work. My first commitment was an in-service session where I learned of Maude's sudden passing, five months short of reaching the century mark. I cried. What poor timing for I wasn't there to sing another song or say how much she meant to

me. The next day I called her daughter and related how much her mother had blessed my life. She already knew.)

"Ivan and the Big Bands"

Ivan survived a 25-year battle with cancer. He had lived on borrowed time for years and outlived most of his doctors. He had a strong will and resiliency seldom seen. He did not talk much and stuck to himself most of the time. Ivan had a musical background and once played fiddle in some big bands in the Chicago area. I'm a big fan of that kind of music and thought how neat to play with such icons as the Dorsey Brothers, Harry James, Russ Morgan and Guy Lombardo.

I introduced myself to Ivan and received less than an enthusiastic response. However, he perked up a little when I told him I played a simulated version of the trumpet and had an interest in big bands. I proceeded to create the instrument. As Ivan looked on with interest, I overlapped my hands and crossed my thumbs to create a small aperture in front. (This cup-like creation can be used to drink water when one doesn't have a glass.) Next, I vocalized through the opening to produce mostly "wah-wahs," and varied the pitch and intonation to simulate a trumpet.

To my surprise, Ivan liked the sound. After the demonstration, I hit the jackpot when I presented a rendition of the Russ Morgan band theme, "Does Your Heart Beat for Me," followed with Clyde McCoy's, "Sugar Blues." As I played, he excitedly jumped to his feet and with an inquisitive look asked, "Where did you learn to do that?" In all humility, I said it evolved with many years of practice. That was the icebreaker. From then on, I could do no wrong.

Ivan invited me to his room to listen to recorded big band music. He had an old stereo console (1960 vintage) that he meticulously prepared to play. In spite of a severe visual impairment, resulting from macular degeneration, he delicately placed a 33 1/3 record of the Harry James Band on the phonograph and positioned the needle in perfect position to begin the concert. When he turned up the volume, a terrific sound ensued. As I enjoyed the music, he asked if I would like a brandy. While flattered and tempted, I politely said, "No thanks—maybe some other time."

During my weekly visits, the routine was always the same. Ivan would request I do my two signature numbers and then we'd listen to big band records from his collection. We felt connected and did not need much conversation to enjoy the moments. The brandy offer was always there, but I never took him up on it.

While Ivan is gone, I have some great memories, all made possible by mutual love for big band music. On occasion, I see Ivan's daughter, who became a hospice volunteer after his death. Every time we chat, I learn more about the special man who became a good friend.

"Jane and Her Flowers"

Jane was a free spirit who loved to talk. Once when asked about her outlook on life, with a smile she stated paradoxically, "I'm even-tempered. I'm always mad." She was never at a loss for words and kept her sense of humor to the end. She had a love for flowers and plants that went beyond the normal attachment. She was always pleased when I delivered weekly summer bouquets from my wife's gardens. After a time, while the flowers lost much of their freshness, Jane saw a beauty not viewed by others and refused to give them up. When asked one day if she wanted the wilted flowers disposed of, she replied, "No! Don't you believe in miracles?"

After several weeks, her room contained many vases of wilted flowers and plants that included an azalea. One day when I took Jane for a walk, Betsy, the housekeeper, cleaned her room and in the process removed the azalea. As Jane enjoyed the fresh air, she reported her daughter would visit that afternoon to claim the azalea plant. Even though the plant had lost much of its beauty, Jane felt TLC would restore and bring it back to life. Subsequently, I made a mad dash to find Betsy who retrieved the plant and returned it to Jane's room. With pride, Jane gave the wilted plant to her daughter. I have often wondered if the plant did in fact live. This incident, while on the humorous side, shows that beauty is in the eyes of the beholder.

Jane had unusual eating habits. When it came to the main course, she was a fussy eater and seldom cleaned her plate. Every now and then, I would encourage her to eat. One day I observed what appeared to be ham and scalloped potatoes on her food tray. Since the food appeared to have been there for a while, I asked if she would like the dish heated up. She gave me the strangest look, and replied, "Why would you want to do that to rhubarb?" I was lost for words and tried to recover from the blunder.

When it came to dessert, Jane loved it all; anything that was sweet pleased her palate. However, she seldom finished the goodies. While she would surrender the unused portion of meat and potatoes, she wanted to keep the fragments of the desserts for future consumption. Much like her obsession to keep flowers past their prime, she also kept desserts when no longer edible. To clear Jane's room of these undesirable items, Betsy and I would form strategies. It represented a challenge that we took seriously. Fortunately, we were generally able to accomplish the feat and still did not alienate our friend.

Another memorable experience took place as Jane and I spent time outside. As we sat on patio chairs near the pond, we watched the mallards dive for prey and the swallows swoop for insects. As we observed the wonders of nature, I informed Jane that deer often came by to feed and drink. No sooner had the words come out of my mouth when a deer appeared. The creature looked us straight in the eye, and proceeded on his journey. Shock and wonderment were in her eyes. She could not figure whether this was a lucky occurrence or whether I was a clairvoyant. Neither could I for that matter. In any case, she had a new found respect for me. As I passed Jane's room, I often overheard this story told to family and friends, each time with a few more embellishments. I chalked up the experience as a typical day as a volunteer and enjoyed the celebrity status.

"Sophie the Gambler and Harry the Hurler"

Sophie and Harry were marriage partners and soul mates for over a half-century. They did everything together and lived life to the fullest. When Sophie became ill, Harry was by her side 24/7. The three of us made an instant connection and became good friends. We shared many of the same interests. I like to gamble, as did Sophie and I love sports, as did Harry; so we had lots to talk about. Each had a delightful sense of humor that came across in our conversations. They were fun people and I looked forward to our visits.

Sophie delighted to tell stories about her escapades on the casino circuit. She relished the times when she won big pots and described techniques to get slot machines to pay off. She recalled a lady who won big on a slot machine. Before the player pulled the lever on the "one armed bandit," she would go through a ritual. First, she rubbed her right hand over the screen, then snapped her finger, and ended as she waived her arms above her head. These weird gyrations got Sophie's attention and many other casino-goers as well. The lady could not lose and emptied the machine several times. Sophie watched until the casino guru left and made a dash for the machine to try her luck. In a close race, she claimed the slot and got ready for action. She used the same preparatory technique as the lady before her, but without the same results. Not only did the machine quit winning, Sophie became physically exhausted and had to cut her casino trip short. The incident taught her to use less rigorous techniques when she played the slots.

One day Sophie left a message for me to see her. As I entered her room, she smiled and pointed to a contraption positioned on the bed stand. You guessed it; it was a slot machine, a gift from the family. I thought, how appropriate. She informed me it was all on the up-and-up and that it did not take money, only tokens. She showed me how to use it and gave a few hints that worked for her. I proceeded to play all 50 tokens week-after-week with little payoff for my efforts. When I suggested she might have tightened the machine, she laughed and said I did not have the right touch. For some reason, Sophie started to receive visits from casual acquaintances and distant relatives, and her room became a popular hangout.

Shortly before Sophie died, her family planned a surprise casino trip as a birthday present. Things could not have turned out any better. She was physically able to tolerate the trip and left the casino a winner. In that she had her day in the sun, she let Harry select the restaurant to celebrate the occasion. He made the most of the opportunity and picked a HOOTER'S establishment. After dinner and four cups of coffee (having never drunk more than two before), Harry reluctantly left the eatery. On the way home, the family teased Harry unmercifully about his choice of restaurants.

Harry was a gifted athlete in his day. In his youth, he excelled as a baseball pitcher and later was a softball hurler well into his fifties. He liked to tell stories about athletic achievements and so did I. We exchanged our nicknames befitting our athletic prowess. I was "Killer" and Harry was "Smokey" (from his legendary pitching exploits on the baseball and softball circuits). He once struck out 17 batters in a single baseball game and earned a place in the town's Hall of Fame. In that I am a sports memorabilia collector, I asked Harry if I might have a baseball picture of him for my collection, to which he happily agreed. We loved to talk about sports, particularly our accomplishments, which became bigger with every passing day.

After Sophie's death, Harry's health failed and he too became a patient at the Home. When wheeled into the facility on a gurney, he gave me a smile, grasped my hand and said, "How are you doing Killer?" We talked sports for the last time. The next day he died. When I returned the next week, there was an envelope with my name on it and inside was a baseball picture of Harry in his prime. The picture is displayed in my sports' gallery at home—a nice remembrance of a wonderful friend.

"Ernie with the Trophy Fish and Gaming Machine"

Ernie was a jovial sort who always had something funny to say. Even though he had an aggressive form of cancer, he never lost his sense of humor. Once when asked, how many children he had, with a deadpan look, he replied, "Three—one of each." To my question, "Do you think I'm a trouble-maker?" He responded, "I don't know about that, but I bet you were a hell-raiser." Our personalities meshed and to tease was fun.

Ernie liked to hear about my flaws and couldn't figure how I had so many. Once I related an incident about my mechanical ineptitude. He listened intently and, between chuckles, shook his head in disbelief as the adventure unfolded. The story goes.

(My mechanical flaws occur even with routine tasks such as to open a door. When we practiced with my barbershop quartet, we alternated homes for rehearsal sites. When we rehearsed at Bob's house (our beloved bass), I dreaded to leave his place for I didn't possess the skills to extricate myself from his home. Said another way, I couldn't open

the door. To release the latch required a series of intricate moves that included one upward, one downward, and one backward. Try as I might I couldn't get the door open. In that I didn't want to fail, at rehearsal's end, I migrated away from the door and hoped that Todd or Ole (my other quartet compatriots) would lead the exit and permit me to follow. In that they knew my ineptitude, they forced me to initiate the series of preparatory tasks and took sadistic pleasure to see me fail. Finally, as they observed my distress, they relented and finally opened the door. While I didn't encounter as much difficulty as I left Todd's or Ole's homes, I preferred to rehearse at my place where I could enter and leave with a modicum of confidence. Bob now has a different home that is user-friendlier. I'm grateful for that.)

Ernie did not think anyone could be that inept and never believed the story. In fact, he didn't believe much of what I said. He should have consulted with Edna ("Edna and the Wheelchair").

Ernie was an outdoor enthusiast who loved to fish and was good at it. He had his own boat and knew the hot spots. Seldom did he go home without a catch. It did not take much to elicit a conversation about his favorite sport. With seldom a pause, he would go on for hours to share stories about the big ones that got away. As he reflected, I visualized Ernie, pole in hand, as he drifted on the lake without a care in the world.

Ernie never said much about the fish he caught. That is with one exception. In his room, he had an 8-pound walleye mounted on the wall. Hardly a day passed when he did not talk about that fish. With pride and a twinkle in his eye, he recreated the catch and described images that defied imagination. Each time he told the story, he added more embellishments as he created a bigger-than-life adventure. As he reminisced about the once-in-a-lifetime experience, for a fleeting moment, he was young and healthy again.

Like Sophie, Ernie also had a slot machine that mysteriously appeared in his room one day. He would not tell from where. When not in use, he kept it covered to disguise the evidence—truly a clandestine operation. It was a fun thing to have and a great conversation piece. I always teased Ernie that it was not in good taste to have the slot machine in a place run by a religious order. With a grin, he revealed his mischievous side and reported several Sisters expressed an interest to play the machine. However, for obvious reasons, they were reluctant participants. However, as he prodded and offered a roll of quarters, occasionally, a dear "Sister," in a moment of weakness, would give in and play. With eager anticipation, she would insert coins and pull the lever only to be disappointed with nothing to show for her investment.

Ernie thought their participation in gaming activities would make good copy (pictures and all) for the local newspaper. That would have made headlines. For the record, there was never any documentation of these episodes. Perhaps they were a figment of Ernie's imagination. In any case, he loved the Sisters and staff for their compassionate care. Our prankish dispositions meshed and we had fun together.

"Millie and Her TV Idol"

Millie, in her mid-90s, led an active, productive life at home. She relished independence and thrived on it. She liked to cook, housekeep and garden. She mowed the grass and shoveled snow. She baby-sat for her great grandchildren. She had a spirited personality, and a sense of humor seldom seen. Her family and friends adored her. While she became seriously ill for the first time, she made a fair adjustment to the change in life style.

When I first met Millie, she was in bed watching T.V. She was enthralled with "The Price is Right" with her idol Bob Barker and did not want to be interrupted. At this critical time, which required all her powers of concentration, she wanted to focus on the show. However, she encouraged me to wait until the show was over when she would have time to talk. Take it or leave it, these were the conditions with no compromises. I accepted them and waited patiently until my turn came. I am glad I did.

Most people, under similar conditions, are self-centered and consumed by their condition—not Millie.

When the television show was over, she turned to me and initiated the conversation. She wanted to know all about me: name, family, job, interests and anything else I wanted to add. I couldn't believe what a selfless person she was and how interested she was in a perfect stranger.

She wanted me to write a biographical sketch and gave me the back of an envelope to do so. She requested her reading glasses and gave me directions on how to fit them with masking tape and rubber bands. It truly was a sight (no pun intended). As I wrote, she would periodically stop me to read the sketch and often asked me to repeat. She was hearing impaired, as most people her age, and wanted to make certain she heard me right. We spent the better part of 30-minutes as she learned about me. She was the person who was sick and in need of support but yet I was the center of attention—what a role reversal.

Later in the day, she requested to see me again. As I entered her room, I observed a different Millie. She had applied a generous amount of makeup with touches of lipstick and eye shadow. A blond wig added to the transformation. Wow! She got my attention. I was flattered and savored the moment. After we stared at each other for a few moments, she requested that I read my biographical sketch again and asked a few more questions about my background. She never gave me a chance to talk about her.

People often know when death is imminent. Call it an intuitive sense. They are comfortable with the thought and look forward to it. Such was the case with Millie. When I said, I would see her next week; she smiled and calmly said, "No, you won't." She died before I had a chance to visit again. In spite of only seeing Millie twice (both in a single day), she left a permanent impression.

"Johnny's Quest for Survival"

The first time I met Johnny he told me his tragic life story as he grew up in the hills of West Virginia. When eleven-years-old, his parents deserted him and left him to fend for himself. To survive, he would wander into the coal mining camps to seek refuge and food. Soon, barely a teenager, he worked in the mines. In spite of inhumane treatment and deplorable working conditions, Johnny persevered. For survival sake, he left the mining country, while still a teen, and lived a nomadic existence. He traveled from state-to-state as rides became available and tried to find his niche.

About twenty years ago, he established roots in Wisconsin. While he had no formal education and was unable to read or write (or so he said), he became street-smart and acquired an education in "hard knocks." He went to rummage and estate sales and knew a bargain when he saw one. He sold his wares, everything from soup-to-nuts (e.g., antique furniture, jewelry, pots and pans, old books and magazines, trading cards, lawn ornaments) at flea markets and lived from hand-to-mouth.

Johnny's forced life style in his early years eventually took a toll on his health. Because of many years in the mines, he developed "black lung disease," that was in the advanced stages when I met him. He never married and had no family other than a sister who he hadn't seen in years. He was a lonely man and craved attention. Johnny had a quick mind, sharp wit and keen insights into people. However, as might be expected, he was cautious to develop relationships. When convinced there was trust and respect, he would let down his guard and have fun.

As our friendship grew, a sense of humor surfaced. He liked to hear about my flaws, particularly the mechanical fiascos and all the embarrassing experiences. Like Ernie ("Ernie with the Trophy Fish and Gaming Machine"), Johnny couldn't figure how a person with my education could be so inept at things and be such a scatterbrain. I assured him it came from years of practice. He laughed at that. These happenings leveled the playing field and brought us closer together. The following experience brought Johnny to his knees with laughter.

(When making pizzas with my barbershop group for a fundraiser, my task was to put a portioned amount of cheese on each pizza until it reached a targeted weight as measured on a scale. In this Kodak moment, I added cheese, but did not see any movement on the scale. After having gone through a bag of cheese and observed an excessively high pile of dairy product on the pie, I initiated a quality control check. Before I completed the check, one

of my co-workers discovered that I neglected to put the pizza on the scale and with glee, told the group of my brain lapse—how humiliating!)

Before Johnny became bedridden, I would drive him home every now and then, so he could check out the homestead, a modest one-room house located on several acres of land in a rural area. He always talked about taking me fishing near his home, where reportedly there were some real trophies. Out of curiosity, I once asked him to show me the "hot spot." He grinned and directed me through a series of winding roads off the beaten track. Finally, a small body of water appeared. It was not much bigger than a large puddle, about 6-inches deep—not what I expected. Maybe it was a dry year. However, Johnny did not give the impression that the makeup of the pond had changed since he last fished it. I have often wondered if he was putting me on. He was crafty and knew a lot more than he'd admit.

For some reason, Johnny always called me "Bill." Initially, I would instruct him to call me Jack, my given name, or by my old football nickname "Killer." However, after several unsuccessful attempts to preserve my identity, I conceded I was "Bill" to him. In an emotional moment, he once gave me a hug and with tears in his eyes said, "I'll never forget what you've done for me "Bill." I looked around for another person but the compliment was for me. I accepted it with gratitude.

"Everything is Wonderful Harry"

Harry was the eternal optimist and thankful to be alive. In spite of illness, every day was good and gratitude abounded. He was still ambulatory and able to leave the Home for short visits with family and friends. He loved to eat and mealtime was a highlight. Everyday, precisely at noon, he would proceed to the kitchen with eager anticipation. Without a word, he would "tackle" dinner and clean his plate while scarcely a morsel remained. He never ate a meal he did not like and was generous in his praise for the cooks. Harry was popular and a big hit with the kitchen staff. On weekends, he would visit his long time girlfriend. When asked, what he liked best about her, coming as no surprise, he replied, "Her cooking!"

Harry had a quiet demeanor. While our conversations were one-sided, we enjoyed each other's company. He was a good listener and semi-amused by my stories—at least most of them. While laughter wasn't Harry's style, he had a good sense of humor and displayed a grin on occasion. When trained, he responded to my "Happy Birthday" greeting and often beat me to the punch. When I said it first, he would give me his best grin and ask, "Where's my present?" To pass time, he would go to the local Wal-Mart store, and "people watch." Although he never confessed, I got the impression he preferred to watch those of the opposite sex and I teased him about it. He was a nice man and easy to like.

"Sister and Everything is Great"

People of faith often maintain positive outlooks on life and eagerly anticipate the life to come. Sister Bernadette truly exemplified this faith and left a legacy. Never have I seen a person with a stronger faith, peace of mind, or sense of humor in the midst of failing health. To the end, life was WONDERFUL.

Sister Bernadette spent over 40-years as a missionary in a deprived area of Nicaragua. She possessed a passion for her work and an infinite faith. In spite of poor living conditions, she thrived and enjoyed life to the fullest and received great satisfaction as she helped others. She brought a love for music and song to her teaching and community life. Sister's ministry touched lives in many ways. Whether Sister Bernadette raised money and got supplies for her needy people or played baseball with the Nicaraguan children, she set an example for others to emulate. She had fun and got people to laugh—sometimes at themselves. People enjoyed her company, and she brought out the best in them.

Sister Bernadette loved Notre Dame football. As a person of faith, when the Fighting Irish scored, she called it a "T.D. Jesus." She loved to eat and always cleaned her plate. Her favorite cuisine was a hotdog with ketchup and a generous portion of raw onions. That is with a glass of wine or some Southern Comfort—for medicinal purposes only. Life was good for this special lady. However, that changed when she became terminally ill with a degenerative neurological disease. Subsequently, Sister Bernadette came to the States for treatment. As her health rapidly deteriorated, she came to the realization that her missionary work in Nicaragua was finished. While she was devastated and found it difficult to accept, she remained the eternal optimist and never complained about her condition. When asked how she felt, her response was always an unequivocal "WONDERFUL." Sister's unwavering faith was truly inspirational and beyond comprehension. In spite of ailing health, she remained active—never missed a mass, participated in social activities and sang at every opportunity.

As Sister Bernadette's condition worsened, her sister Emma, also a Religious Sister, moved from another state to help with her care. In visits with the Sisters, we shared a mutual interest in music and liked to sing the old songs. They grew up in a musical family. As children, Bernadette, Emma, and their sisters Elca and Maria, would gather around the piano with their father and sing in close harmony. They smiled as they reflected how high their father's standards were and that less than perfect harmony was unacceptable. The bar was set high and there was pressure to please dad.

When they learned I was from Ohio, the Sisters said that I probably knew the old classic "Just a Letter from Ohio." When I said I had never heard of it, they looked in disbelief and my credibility took a hit. How could one that knew so many of the old songs not be familiar with "Just a Letter from Ohio?" Timidly, I said I would be happy to learn it. At first, I did not think they would take time to teach me. However, they relented, and true to their father's style, put me through the paces. I too felt the pressure they experienced as children but persevered to master the song. As we practiced, they were equally surprised how fast I picked up the harmony and how slowly I learned the words—a real paradox. Eventually, the song did become a favorite and usually started our weekly songfests. Our trio became a favorite of the staff and patients in the nursing home. Once we tried to capitalize on our fame, after a stellar performance of "Just a Letter from Ohio," and passed around the hat. To our dismay, we only got 27 cents. After a short discussion, we agreed to keep our amateur status.

In spite of Sister Bernadette's ailing health and weakened state, she wanted to sing when I visited and did so until her voice gave out. At her funeral prayer service, her family asked me to sing some songs from our repertoire. I asked Emma, Elca and Maria to join me in singing "When You're Smiling." As we held hands, the quartet performed in Sister Bernadette's honor. With a little celestial help, it never sounded better. Next, the sisters wanted me to join them in "Just a Letter from Ohio." I was reluctant to do so because of my inability to remember the words. However, in a moment of weakness, I consented to do so. Remarkably, for the first time, I remembered all the words—a miracle no less. The 4-part harmony was great and we heard overtones that sounded like Sister Bernadette. As we smiled collectively, we all looked up and saluted her.

At Sister Bernadette's funeral, many spoke on her behalf and shared fond memories—many on the light side. I learned one of her favorite FUN songs was "Ninety-Nine Bottles of Beer on the Wall." It goes: "Ninety-nine bottles of beer on the wall and if one of those bottles of beer should fall, we would have ninety-eight bottles of beer on the wall." Emma related that Bernadette would do all ninety-nine verses in a single session. Had I known this was a favorite song of hers, we could have incorporated it into our repertoire—at least a shortened version.

Sister Bernadette was a dog lover and while no longer able to have the real thing at the nursing home, she had a toy basset hound that provided some companionship without the barking. As she always rooted for the under-dog (another pun), Sister liked that breed of dog with sad face, droopy ears and crooked legs.

As Emma, Elca and Maria left the cemetery after Sister's burial, a dog suddenly appeared along the side of the road, a basset hound no less. Instinctively, they stopped the car, rolled down the windows and focused on the animal. The dog looked them straight in the eye, barked a couple of times and slowly walked away. They could only imagine the significance of the event. Could it have been Sister Bernadette, incognito, letting them know everything was okay?

Several weeks after the death of Sister Bernadette, I had a great visit with Emma who reflected on the Christ-like life of her beloved sister, and the anticipation to see her again. She related how happy memories kept her going. With a smile, she talked about Bernadette's childhood and what a "tomboy" she was. On one occasion, the family (minus Bernadette) was at the supper table. Suddenly, the girls' father jumped up from the table, grabbed a rifle and made a quick exit outside. The sound of gunshots ensued and the family, for fear of their lives, took cover. A few minutes later, Bernadette entered the kitchen, white as a sheet, followed by her father. It turned out that Bernadette, along with some of her boy chums, had climbed the large cherry tree in the backyard (a definite no-no) to pick the red delicacies. To get their attention, dad delivered a couple of shots in the air. The attention-getter worked effectively and the group set a record as they extricated themselves from the tree. Word has it they all felt blessed to still be alive. Because of the divine intervention, Bernadette made a vow to become a Sister. That is probably not true, but it makes a good story.

Before I left my visit with Sister Emma, she requested we again sing, "Just a Letter from Ohio." During the song, just like the funeral service, another part was present— déjà vu. We thanked Sister Bernadette.

"Oscar's Special Friends"

(It is frequent for patients to develop a strong dependence with others. In Oscar's case, he craved constant companionship. It just so happened he preferred the female variety, although I did sneak in at the end. He found solace because the ladies treated him special and cared for him unconditionally. This type of caring is common in hospice work and helps patients, such as Oscar, make the most of their final days.)

Initially, Oscar was ambulatory and required minimal assistance to carry out daily activities unless accompanied by a companion of the opposite sex. When alone, Oscar would take rigorous walks with perfect posture and seldom a limp. However, when a lady appeared, he would bend over, shuffle his feet and require considerable assistance to move about. He would grasp the chosen's arm and struggle to take a step, and the walk from the parlor to his room became an arduous activity. When the person left the area, much to his dismay, he would return to the parlor in half the time. Later, Oscar insisted a lady have lunch with him. To fit the occasion, he would dress in his Sunday best. With a dapper look, he would arrive early in the kitchen and request another place setting next to his. When the lady arrived, his eating habits changed and he required assistance. If one of his lady friends failed to show for lunch, Oscar was all business. He would fend for himself and was the first to leave the table.

Oscar frequently moved about the residence as he looked bored and craved companionship. As he meandered, I offered to walk with him. He generally responded with a sullen look and said, "I don't think so—not today." Shortly after, when he received the same offer from a lady, Oscar transformed. He took on a happy face and readily accepted. Soon the couple, hand-in-hand, appeared outside for a garden walk. There was Oscar in all his glory as he displayed his best shuffle. When there were no offers, he became assertive and requested a female staff member (the younger the better) to take him for a walk. If too busy to do so, Oscar moped and headed towards his room. I once heard him say, with a sullen look, "That woman broke my heart."

I was not one of Oscar's favorites. He once asked me what I had done for a living. When I replied, a college professor, he looked surprised, said that was hard to believe and wondered if they (meaning the powers that be) asked me to leave. While in shock, I had no response. Still I searched for a compliment and asked if he enjoyed my singing (not good judgment on my part). He immediately responded, "No!"

To better understand what made Oscar tick, I asked what he liked to do. He quickly responded, "Nothing. That's what I do best." As I tried to make conversation, I inquired how many children he had. Without hesitation, he said, "About four." How does one respond to that?

I continued to offer my services as I hoped to establish a connection. Over time, he could no longer walk and, with reluctance, agreed to a wheelchair. One day when I asked how he was, he responded with a grin (a first for me) "fair-to-middlin." His words threw me for a loop for I didn't know what they meant and didn't have the courage to ask. His compliant behavior suggested he might be doing okay, but I wasn't certain and had to find out. After my tour of duty, I made a quick exit and drove the 20 miles to my place in record time (perhaps some exaggeration here). I entered my home without a word, ran to the den, sat down at the computer and Googled "fair to middlin." I found it is a term that comes from grades of cotton with "middling" being the best grade. So if someone asks how you are, it is somewhere between average or better—a positive occurrence. I was thrilled for Oscar's sake. While he still preferred help from the opposite gender, we no longer had barriers and, in a pinch, let me take him for a walk.

One day Oscar revealed a caring, sensitive side. As I negotiated his wheelchair around the grounds and up an incline, he observed my labored breathing and expressed concern I might be overdoing it. I thanked him, gasped for air and proceeded with the walk at a slower pace. As we descended the hill, Oscar expressed another concern. With the semblance of a smile, mixed with a look of panic, he said, "Don't let go!" I laughed and firmly grasped the handles on the wheelchair. There was humor.

After that incident, our relationship became stronger. One day when I greeted Oscar in the dining room over lunch, he put his arm on my shoulder and said, "You are a comfort." As I fought back tears, I thanked him and regained my composure. I last saw Oscar when he was comatose. As I sat at his bedside, I stroked his hand and told his son and daughter of warm moments shared with their dad.

"Dear Lady from England"

(It's one thing to be selfless when healthy but quite another when terminally ill for there is a natural tendency to be absorbed with self. This sketch involves a patient whose unconditional caring for others never changed during illness.)

Ruth, a native of England, came to this country as a young adult. She was proud of her heritage and had a delightful accent to show for it. She had been a stay-at-home mom and raised three terrific children. She lived for family and nothing else mattered. When one of her sons visited her, I commented what a good mother he had. His response, "I have a GREAT mother!"

When I met Ruth, she was ambulatory and able to care for herself. With her positive outlook on life and selfless concern for others, she picked up the spirits of patients as well as staff. She loved to give to others. Once when concerned that some patients would not have company for

Easter, she purchased a ham so they could have a special dinner.

Ruth was a great conversationalist and liked to share her sense of humor. She related an incident that happened in the dining area around lunchtime. In that Ruth was a new resident, she didn't know all the dining protocols. Unsure of herself, she timidly sat down at the buffet in front of a table setting. Shortly thereafter, a lady entered the room, gave Ruth a stern look and, without uttering a word, moved the utensils to another area on the table. As Ruth tried to recover from the shock, she expressed deep concern whether she was welcome and most importantly, whether she would get something to eat.

Later Ruth learned why the incident occurred and jovially talked about it. The lady, who had removed Ruth's table setting, was the spouse of a patient who had been at the Home for an extended period. She and her husband had a routine to eat at the same place at the table and were not flexible to change. Once Ruth realized the situation, she had no hang-ups where to sit and enjoyed the couple's company.

Ruth made the meal a pleasurable experience for all at the table. She always praised Phyllis, the cook, about how great the food looked and tasted. Respectful to her heritage, tea and crumpets (a special order) were included in the meals. The dining experience was a highlight of Ruth's day.

Ruth gave a spirit and life that brought out the best in everyone. Even until a couple days before her death, she was still able to move about and carry on those signature conversations that entertained so many. To the end, Ruth made the best of a compromised life and was grateful for the hospice experience.

"Sara and the Organ Music"

Before her illness, Sara lived an active life and was committed to helping others. She raised three children as a single parent and later went to college to become a social worker. She had good taste and enjoyed pleasant surroundings. Her room was a show place. A wide array of Tiffany lamps created a panorama of color and relaxed atmosphere that was a nice site for a visit.

Sara liked all forms of music and loved to play the organ. On my weekly visits, Sara and I would sing a few of the old songs in the ambience of her room and then proceed to the parlor where she played the organ. She would leaf through her favorite songbook to search for the perfect number that she could play and I could sing. The selection process was an arduous task and matching our skills represented a challenge. A major obstacle was to get the tonal key that would accommodate my vocal range. It seemed the key Sara selected was either too low and or too high (even in my falsetto register) to sing comfortably. However, she showed an inordinate amount of tolerance for my limitations and searched carefully for the optimal starting point.

Once we selected the song, we practiced diligently. When we hit some clunkers (a frequent occurrence on my part), we would start again hoping to advance a little further. In that it took so many repeats to get through a single song, we became the butt of jokes (me more so than Sara). Perhaps that's a bit strong, but when people asked for earplugs, we sensed a lack of appreciation for our music. However, we remained undaunted and with a smile, continued in the quest for perfection.

In those short periods when the music was REALLY GOOD (at least in our minds), activity stopped and people, in an apparent state of shock, listened and even applauded. At these times, Sara and I were ecstatic, and smiled right on key (pun intended). It was so nice to have the effort rewarded. At these special times, I would blurt out, "I don't want to brag or anything, but I think that's the best we ever did it." These happy moments consumed Sara and created positive energy.

"Vernice and the One Man Band"

Vernice was a private person, but enjoyed a circle of friends, some of them hospice volunteers, who visited her on a daily basis. She craved companionship and relished the support. She loved fluffy toy animals and had a menagerie in her room. Each critter had its place of honor.

When one was out of position, she moved it to its rightful place.

One day I came upon a toy bunny which was a table decoration in the kitchen. Immediately, I thought of Vernice and took the fluffy creature for her to see. As I entered the room, her eyes fixated on the animated bunny. As it moved its ears and waved its paws with the music, Vernice would slide her feet and nodded her head with approval. Unfortunately, I had to return the animal to its place in the kitchen. With the realization that Vernice liked music, we sang a number of the old songs. She would smile ever so slightly and softly sing along.

The following week I had a Stumpf Fiddle in the car having played it the night before at a quartet sing-out. *(Note: The folk instrument, named after peg leg Harry Stumpf, is common in Wisconsin and featured at polka fests and barroom singing. It consists of a long wooden stick with a rubber ball attached to the base. Also attached are two pie tins (with some un-popped popcorn inside), two door springs across the pan, a breadboard and a cowbell. To play, the would-be musician bounces the stick in rhythm to the song and with a drumstick, creates music by striking the assorted noisemakers.)*

The thought suddenly occurred Vernice might enjoy a song or two with this unique instrument. In that I didn't want to run the risk of being in poor taste, I consulted with Sister Sue to get approval. She gave me permission to proceed with two stipulations: to keep the noise down and not get too carried away. I accepted the conditions and, with eager anticipation, prepared for the performance with a five-minute rehearsal in the parking lot.

As I entered Vernice's room with the strange contraption, she looked bewildered and asked what it was. I obliged with a detailed description that I cut short when she began to doze. After I got her attention, I began a demonstration to prepare for the performance. I clutched the top of the instrument firmly with a grip of the left hand and placed it in a resting position on the floor. I then grabbed the drumstick with my right hand. I was ready. Vernice was all eyes and ears. With a vigorous up and down movement of my left hand and arm, I bounced the machine off the floor with the action of the rubber ball. The resultant sound as it hit the floor, along with the random movement of the popcorn in the pie tins, was music to behold. When the bouncing was rhythmically in synch, I struck the noisemakers sequentially with the drum stick—first the springs, then the cowbell and finally the breadboard and prepared to sing with self-accompaniment. This represented a challenge for a guy "who can't walk and chew gum at the same time."

With the preliminaries completed, I sensed Vernice was ready for a little entertainment and wasn't disappointed. I searched for the optimal pitch to get the polka favorite, "Just Because," in my limited vocal range. When successful, I began to sing with my faithful instrument. The music got Vernice's attention and a marked transformation occurred. Call it surprise, fascination, or a little bit of both; she was a different person with no inhibitions   Excitedly, Vernice lifted her feet several inches from the floor and stomped vigorously to the rhythm of the music. Her performance attracted attention and soon her room was full of well-wishers. We all loved the new Vernice and did a couple of more numbers until she became exhausted.

As Vernice's health deteriorated, she knew her time was near. During the last weeks, she was not able to achieve inner peace and was fearful of dying. I visited Vernice the last time when she was in a semi-comatose state. As she moaned softly, she received comfort from Mary, a volunteer friend. However, when I entered her room, she smiled and firmly grasped my hand. Mary reported Vernice playfully talked about my previous visits (the episode with the bunny and the shenanigans with the one-man band) and thought I was a real "nut." What a neat compliment! As Mary and I continued to talk, Vernice, during a lucid moment, smiled and suddenly began to move her arms up and down as if she were playing the instrument. What a remarkable reaction, for this lady, even as death drew near, enjoyed a happy moment and displayed a sense of humor. I sensed Vernice had found inner peace. She died the following day.

"Marty the Consummate Musician"

Marty was a distinguished individual with lots of class. He had a polished speaking voice, a captivating personality and was a great conversationalist. He was a successful businessman and an accomplished musician. For years, he owned and managed a top-of-the-line shoe store. He also played saxophone and clarinet in house bands when many of the elite groups came to Milwaukee (e.g., the Dorseys, Glenn Miller, Harry James, Guy Lombardo). In addition, he hosted a popular radio show that featured big band music. In his room was an impressive collage of pictures that highlighted his career. The collage attracted many female viewers who recognized him as a "hunk" in his day. In spite of his illness, he still possessed a charm that he readily shared. He was fun to visit and I felt good in his presence. I always got the idea he was the giver and I the receiver. However, I hope he received something good from my visits as well.

When I first met Marty, I shared my interest in music in general and big bands in particular. As I did with Ivan ("Ivan and the Big Bands"), I did an impromptu performance on my hand trumpet featuring "Sugar Blues," and "Does Your Heart Beat for Me." While not as impressed with my musical skills as was Ivan, Marty gave me a polite thumbs-up. However, I got the idea that my performance to him lacked skill and professionalism. He was perceptive. Still as I tried to impress, I switched from my hand trumpet to a vocal rendition of some old songs. Unfortunately for me, his reaction to "My Wild Irish Rose," and "Down by the Old Mill Stream," drew a tepid response at best.

In a subtle way, Marty reminded me to be less of a performer and more of a listener. When he asked if I would like to hear some of his big band tapes, I responded with an enthusiastic "YES!" He made his point, and I learned my lesson. As we listened to the tapes, he smiled and beat time to the music. His eyes drifted to a different time and place. He had returned to the 50s enjoying what he did best.

"Sharing a Nickname—Henry and Me"

(Visits from grandchildren are special and bring another perspective to life that is vibrant and energizes patients with terminal illness. Further, their honesty, innocence and absence of agendas help develop special relationships. This story reflects the pride a grandfather had for a grandson.)

Shortly after Henry arrived, we had a pleasant conversation. While he was not a man of many words, we connected with our mutual interest in sports and as avid Packer fans. As we spoke, he showed me a personalized picture from a Packer player autographed to "Killer," his nickname and surprisingly mine too. When I inquired how he got his nickname, he just smiled and changed the subject. I wondered if it involved a bloodcurdling story. I can only speculate.

Without any prodding, I shared the history of my nickname. As Henry listened to my story, he grinned and shook his head in disbelief. With lots in common, he and I became good friends. We would always greet each other with our nickname followed by a vigorous handshake. It bonded one "Killer" to another. We would then share highlights of last week's Packer game or some other sporting event and, as "armchair quarterbacks," would offer critical analyses.

While the Packers made for great conversation, Henry preferred to talk about his grandson Sam who played football at a local college. Sam had a wonderful relationship with his grandfather and visited him often. Their time together was therapeutic. Henry prominently displayed Sam's football picture next to his bed, while the picture of the Packer player was in the corner of the room. There was no doubt which player was the star—at least in Henry's eyes. The simple formula for getting Henry to talk was to mention Sam, and he would proceed to boast about his grandson's accomplishments both on and off the gridiron.

Even as Henry's condition weakened in his latter days, he always greeted me with a smile and a "Hello Killer." To the end, he had a FIRM handshake. We had a real connection and enjoyed sharing nicknames.

"Hazel and the Silent Movies"

At 101, Hazel possessed a feisty spirit and mental alertness seldom seen in people half her age. Under five feet and weighing less than 100 pounds, she was a shining example that good things come in small packages. She always spoke her piece and there never was a doubt what was on her mind.

What an interesting background Hazel had. Her daughter, always by her side, beamed with pride as she shared stories about her beloved mother. Hazel was quite a musician in her day and as an 18-year-old, played organ at a local theatre during silent movies until the talkies arrived. In her room was a framed photograph of her at the console—a lasting remembrance. After her music days, she worked in the local drugstore where she served sodas and consumed more than her share of ice cream.

Hazel had a love for life and work ethic that made people take notice. Even in her 80s, she did all the housework, mowed the yard, shoveled snow, did the cooking (made pies to die for), and changed storm windows. Her family adored her and she them. At family gatherings, she was the life of the party, particularly when she consumed a brandy old fashion or two.

As a senior, Hazel remained an avid Packers fan and had an intense hatred for the dreaded Chicago Bears. When she heard that former Bear quarterback Jim McMahon signed with the Packers as a backup to Brett Favre, she wrote a terse letter to Packer CEO Bob Harlan. Hazel expressed disappointment and threatened to change her allegiance. How could the Packers make such a move? Vince Lombardi would turn over in his grave she thought.

Hazel was also a Brewers fan. While she did not have the passion she had with the Packers, she was still an ardent fan. When Hazel reached the century milestone, Bob Uecker, "Mr. Baseball" and the radio voice of the Brewers, congratulated her on this achievement and for her loyalty.

The first time I met Hazel she was eating dinner with assistance from her daughter Jan. This tiny lady's voracious appetite caught my attention. She consumed moderate helpings of roast beef, mashed potatoes and peas and still had room for dessert. I looked on with amazement as she accomplished the feat nonstop without saying a word.

After she completed the feast, I introduced myself to her as "Jack the volunteer." She inquired what I wanted and why I was there—reasonable questions for an uninvited guest. I responded that I was there to say hello and sing her a song. While Hazel was not overly receptive to the idea, her daughter gave me encouragement. As I held her hand, I proceeded to sing "When You're Smiling." As I sang, Hazel's handgrip became firmer and you could tell she was really into the music. When I omitted a word, she quickly filled in the appropriate one—much to the amazement of her family and to me I might add. To my astonishment, Hazel had a strong, booming voice low in pitch—most likely a bass in her day. How could the strong, robust voice come from such a little lady who had lived for over a century?

I felt an instant connection with Hazel. Regardless of her mood and condition, she gave me a pleasant greeting. While she did not always remember my name by immediate recall, she could always pick it out from a multiple choice set. I became extremely fond of Hazel and looked forward to our time together. My visits with her and Jan were upbeat and refreshing. We sang old songs together (as she recalled segments of the lyrics) and made small talk about happy things. When I told Hazel, she was in the book I was writing, she responded, with a hint of a smile, "Hope not." However, I got the impression she liked the idea. Before I left, I would give her an affectionate peck on the cheek and she would respond, "Thank you." How neat was that! She knew how to make a guy feel good. What a special lady she was.

The week before Hazel died she was especially alert and in good spirits. She smiled, was conversant, displayed her wit and sang several songs with me. I left Hazel's room that day with a warm feeling that I shared with her daughter. To my surprise, the next week she was gone. I am convinced our last visit was Hazel's way of saying goodbye in a rousing manner.

"Barry the Baseball Authority"

(The substance of this sketch (with lots of names and statistics) relates to people with a passionate/obsessive interest in sports—in this case major league baseball. They excel at name-dropping and are always available to talk trivia. Barry and I fit the mold having spent hours with the obsession (how fortunate for both of us). I include the vignette to show how Barry's mindset changed as he talked baseball. The dialogue shows a different person, not consumed by illness, as he relived his childhood days on the sandlot. I shared in his "Field of Dreams.")

One day, when I arrived for my weekly visit, a staff nurse, who knew I was a huge sports fan, wanted me to meet Barry, a new patient, who had an interest in baseball. When I entered Barry's room, a wide array of books caught my attention. As I took a closer look, I realized the entire library was about baseball. After a brief introduction, we talked baseball nonstop for better than an hour. During our discussion, Barry really perked up. Baseball took precedence and nothing else mattered. We both had the time of our lives as we shared knowledge of the game and recalled some of the legends.

Barry quickly let me know he was a Chicago Cub's fan. When I directed his attention to the club's collapse in 1969, as most loyal Cub fans, he was not discouraged and optimistic that a pennant was near. I really got his attention when I rattled off the Cub's infield that year:

(Rod Hundley—catcher, Ron Santo—3rd base, Don Kessinger—shortstop, Glenn Beckert—2nd base and Ernie Banks ("Mr. Cub")—1st base).

Next, I shared experiences as a Cleveland Indian's fan that grew up in Ohio and tried to impress him with what I knew about their winning the World Series in 1948. Little did I know I had met my match. He corrected me on a number of incidents I thought to be factual. I told him Larry Doby, the first African-American to play in the American League, came to the big leagues in 1948 (11 weeks after Jackie Robinson broke the color barrier in the National League). However, he let me know, in no uncertain terms, it was in 1947 and offered to give documentation from his baseball encyclopedia. I was in error again when I said Al Rosen was the Indian's third baseman in 1948. As he gloated, he reminded me it was Kenny Keltner and, for good measure, related he was a Milwaukee native.

Barry was also an avid Milwaukee Braves fan and his favorite player in that era was their first baseman Joe Adcock—a switch hitter. I suggested that "Big Joe" was one of the best power hitters ever. Barry agreed with Adcock's prowess when he hit from the left side but as a batter from the right side was a weak hitter. "Three strikes and you're out." Barry dominated and I went back to the drawing board.

On another visit, I brought some of my sports memorabilia to show Barry and hoped to impress him. The items included a model of the catcher's mitt worn by the Indian's Jim Hegan, in the late 40s and early 50s, when he caught the "Big Four"—Bob Feller, Early Wynn, Bob Lemon and Mike Garcia. Before I had a chance to show Barry what I knew about this group of baseball legends, he stole my thunder and recited many of their vital statistics. He reminded me that Hegan, although a weak hitter was a great defensive catcher, and that the "Big Four" consistently totaled over 75 wins a season.

I gave it my best hit (pun intended) and tried to impress Barry with my prized possession, an Indian's scorebook from 1953. As a 14-year-old fan with a passion for the game, I diligently listened to the Indian games on the radio and recorded the results of each player's at-bat. As I looked through the scorebook, I singled (another pun) out some featured games, and reviewed batting stats of some star players. Initially, Barry was impressed.

In that I only had the last names of the players recorded in the scorebook, I requested Barry give me their first names—a challenge I thought. Again, I was wrong. To Smith, Avila, Doby and Rosen, he quickly responded correctly, Al, Bobby, Larry and Al. I could not catch him up on anything. He grinned and enjoyed the moment.

The book included a score sheet of the major league all-star game played on July 14, 1953, won by the National League 5-1. As we reviewed the players, we came across the name of Ted Kluszewski, a big power slugger, who played first base for the Cincinnati Reds. Barry related a remarkable statistic about Kluszewski. "Big Klu" had more home runs than strike outs, an unusual occurrence for power hitters who strike out frequently. In fact, he had 40 home runs in 1953 while he only struck out 34 times. When I challenged Barry to give authenticity, he went directly to *The Baseball Encyclopedia* and provided documentation. Finally, the light came on with the realization I was out of my league.

The following week Barry gave me another bit of trivia. He related that Joe Sewell, a shortstop for the Cleveland Indians in the 20s and 30s only struck out 114 times in over 7000 at-bats in his 14-year career. That is an impressive statistic for many of today's players strike out every 4-5 times at-bat. In that Barry was convinced I was also obsessed with baseball statistics, he offered me one of his cherished encyclopedias, knowing that it wouldn't collect dust. I thanked him for his generosity and told him how much I wanted the book, but only if I could pay for it. We negotiated a deal and I am now the proud owner of a piece of baseball history and have a wonderful remembrance of Barry.

With pride and regret, Barry showed me a draft of a manuscript of his book on baseball. It gave the vital statistics of major league players going back over 50 years sorted out by their native states. The Wisconsin group included such baseball luminaries as Kenny Keltner, Harvey Kuenn, Tony Kubeck, Bob Uecker and Jimmy Gantner.

What an impressive document it was. Unfortunately, Barry knew he would not live to see the book published.

As a footnote, Barry started collecting baseball cards in the third grade, a hobby that carried on for a lifetime. He loved to play the game and in his youth was an outstanding player. As he talked about his exploits on the sandlots, he proudly showed me a trophy that he won as a 10-year-old prep league all-star. Baseball was bigger than life for Barry. Talking about THE GAME represented a great way to connect with him. It was wonderful to see Barry so happy and passionate about a cause. It rubbed off on me.

Barry rarely displayed outward emotion and seldom smiled. I took on the challenge to see if I could get him to smile or even laugh. It had to be about baseball. After an exhaustive search in my sports collection, I came across the Abbot and Costello animated figurine in my sports collection of the classic "Who's on First" baseball routine.

*(In this routine, Abbot identifies the players of a baseball team position-by-position. For example, the first baseman's name is **Who** and the shortstop's is **I Don't Give a Darn**. However, the names of the players expectedly confuse Costello. The dialogue begins with the first baseman **Who**. When Costello asks Abbot who's on first, Abbot quickly responds he's correct **Who** is in fact on first. In utter frustration, Costello reiterates that he's the one asking who's on first, Abbot again responds, that's*

his name. The exchange continues with Costello, who be-
comes even more confused with the introduction of other
players. Costello becomes more infuriated and finally, at
his wits end, says he doesn't give a darn.. Abbot responds
that's the name of the shortstop ending the skit.)

As Barry watched the animation and listened to this classic, a large smile appeared followed by laughter. He had passed the litmus test. I said little and savored the moment.

"Teresa and the Family Songfests"

My first and only experience with Teresa, her husband Elmer, other family members and friends was a memorable one. As I entered Teresa's room, about a dozen people greeted me. In view of the congestion, I thought it might be more appropriate for me to leave and return at another time. However, the group insisted I stay, and am glad I did. I gave my standard introduction as a hospice volunteer and assured Teresa's entourage she would receive the very best care from a devoted staff.

I learned that Teresa and Elmer had been married for 66 years. With pride, they talked about family—6 children, 12 grandchildren and 5 great grandchildren. It did not take long to know how devoted they were to each other and what a wonderful union they had. You could see it in their eyes. As we talked, it was obvious they were on the same page and in total synch. When I asked Elmer if he had any hobbies, with an affectionate smile, he pointed to Teresa and said, "She is!" In spite of Teresa's ill health, she still displayed a delightful sense of humor and an eternal optimism—attributes shared by Elmer. I thought this was a union made in heaven.

I took Teresa's hand and sang "When You're Smiling." Right on cue, she smiled, and not content to only listen, sang along. She had a great alto voice and sang in perfect harmony. Shortly thereafter, everyone else got into the act and a chorus ensued. The harmonious sound of the group rang down the halls and people gathered to hear. The power of music was never more evident. During the hour-long songfest, we sang such standards, as "My Wild Irish Rose," "I've Been Working on the Railroad" and "You are My Sunshine," that never sounded better. As I left, there was a chorus of applause and smiles. The group interaction through music was a wonderful way to connect.

While Teresa died before I returned the next week, my brief time with her, Elmer and the family left a deep-rooted impression. A lot of living was crammed into an hour, and I felt blessed to have been a part of it.

"Alexia and Her Family of Teachers"

At 89 years of age and in declining health, Alexia still possessed a feisty spirit. Without reservation, she offered opinions with no compromises. She called an ace-an-ace and a spade-a-spade. There was nothing subtle about her.

Alexia taught school for 37 years, many in the inner city, and was proud of her life as an educator. She began her career in a one-room schoolhouse where she taught all grades. She accepted life's challenges and passed them on to her three daughters. Due to their mother's influence, all became teachers. This pleased Alexia and she freely boasted about their accomplishments.

The day I met Alexia, she was bedridden. She did not take kindly to her sickness and fatigue. In fact, she lamented that all she did was sleep. What a waste of time she thought. When we were together, she tried to stay awake and wanted to talk. When she did converse, a strong-will prevailed.

Once Alexia initiated the conversation and asked why I was there. I responded that as a volunteer, I just stopped by to say hello. She mellowed immediately and with a smile said, "That's about the nicest thing that you could say." When asked, after the fact, if it was okay to sit down, she, with a look of indifference, responded, "You sat!" She became skeptical as I asked questions about her life history. She wondered why I asked the questions and what my motives were. I assured her they were honorable. She accepted the explanation for a short time. However, her mood changed suddenly when I asked if she enjoyed her career as a teacher. She responded indignantly, "What kind of question is that?" She then followed with a piercing voice that rang down the hall, "You bet your sweet "bippy!"(*I googled "bippy" and found this colloquial expression, not in the dictionary, is a "jocular euphemism" for ones posterior—popularized by comedian icons Rowan and Martin.*) Her response caught me off guard. I wondered where this little lady, so weak from illness, got the energy, let alone passion, to respond in such a manner. Wow! I thought.

Alexia's daughter Jill shared life experiences of her mother and showed me scrapbooks of her 80th and 85th birthday parties. Here are some quotes that exemplified her strong will and feisty spirit. "Quit your belly aching." "Come again before that one gets old." "I'll give you something to cry about." "Stop all that monkey business." "Great minds run in the same family." "One of these times—Pow! Pow! Pow!—right in the kisser."

When I visited Alexia, she would always greet me in a different way, and I was not always sure that she recognized me from week-to-week. Once she gave me a strange look and asked, "Did you lose weight or change brothers?" I assured her I was not my brother and, since I was on a diet, thanked her for the compliment. I asked if she minded if I sang her a "golden oldie." Although not overly excited by the request, she agreed. When I questioned how she liked the song, she quickly responded that it was too long. That really hurt, for even the long version of "When You're Smiling" lasts less than 30 seconds. I then made some small talk about the weather and other mundane things. Alexia gave me a look of disgust and indicated she had no idea where I was going with the conversation. She was right. I didn't. She always kept me on my toes.

Alexia not only had a passion for teaching but for bowling as well. As a young adult, she excelled at the sport and had a 299 game to show for it. She even received an invitation to go on the professional tour. While she never accepted the offer, she loved to talk about it. When I asked if she recognized some of the bowling icons of the past, such as Don Carter, Billy Welu and Don Weber, she responded, that was a silly question and of course she knew who they were. Later, she became actively involved in the junior bowling program and was an instructor for over 30 years. I thought of the old adage, "Once a teacher always a teacher."

At the tender age of 65 years, Alexia bought her own horse and took up horseback riding. When I indicated how impressed I was she'd taken up the sport in her senior years, she responded, "What's so unusual about that?" Age had no barriers and moderation did not fit her style. She did it all and lived to tell about it. When I referred to her as a matriarch, a compliment I thought, she gave me a stern look and said that was one of her most <u>unfavorable</u> words. While I failed again, I loved her style.

One day as she was cared for by staff, Alexia expressed discontent and was cantankerous. When put back in bed, she requested my presence—what an honor I thought. As I entered her room, she smiled warmly and grasped my hand firmly. She did not want me to leave. For the first time, I saw the warm, tender side of Alexia and felt a real connection. She wanted me to sing, and we had a marvelous songfest. As I sang the old songs, she was relaxed and contented. She mouthed the words and directed as she waved her arms.

The next week Alexia was in a semi-comatose state. I had a lengthy talk with Jill who was always there for her mother. I told her what a wonderful daughter she had been. She needed to hear that, particularly from an outsider. Jill indicated that some of the most meaningful moments shared with her mother occurred during her illness. She recorded these treasures and included many humorous one-liners for posterity. I stood by Jill's side, stroked Alexia's arm and sang "When You're Smiling." Her eyes opened slightly in response to the music. She smiled and nodded her head—what a touching moment. Alexia died a few days later.

"Iron Man Duke"

My time with Duke represented yet another experience with sports that formed a bond. While I only saw him on two occasions before he died, I got to know him well and had great fun as we talked about sports—particularly baseball.

While Duke was a confirmed bachelor, he was quite social and enjoyed people. He had lots of extended family that lived nearby and many friends. He had a small farm where he raised crops and milked a few cows. While he lived modestly, he had all he needed and was content with life.

Duke had a passion to play baseball. As a teenager, he played on some elite teams that competed around the state. His long, lanky frame was ideal for first base. He usually got "wood on the ball" and seldom struck out. Through the years, while his peers retired from the game, Duke continued to play. In his 40s, he switched from baseball to softball where he often outperformed players half his age. He played slow pitch softball well into his 70s, not in senior leagues but in regular adult leagues where the competition was keen.

I saw Duke in the latter stages of illness when he needed assistance with all activities of daily life. I saluted him for his prowess as a ball player and told him of my interest in the game. He smiled gratefully, as "old jocks" do, and our day began. As I fed him lunch, we had a great talk about the sorry state of modern day baseball. He detested the multi-million dollar contracts that many players receive for less than stellar performances, and how the life and passion for the game have disappeared. Duke's nephew also got into the discussion, and we shared stories. As we talked, a transformation occurred. Duke perked up, sat with perfect posture, his voice became stronger and a renewed spirit appeared. He generously offered his opinions that included a few expletives. He was in his element and loved every minute of the conversation.

When I returned the next week, Duke was comatose. His extended family, that included two brothers, a sister, two nephews, and a niece were by his side. I talked about the special time Duke and I had the week before. They reminisced and recalled many fond memories that included some about his favorite pass-time. As I left the room, I offered my respects. About ten minutes later, the "Divine Umpire" intervened.

"Selfless Bea"

While Bea was unable to care for her basic needs, she was mentally alert and conversant. By nature, she was selfless and committed to caring for family. Nothing else mattered. As I entered her room, a gallery of family pictures caught my eye and a warm spirit prevailed. As Bea proudly showed me the pictures, she introduced each of her nine children, all highly successful physicians and attorneys. What pleased her most were their work ethic and passion to help others. One of her sons was a local ear specialist that I worked with professionally for a number of years. While we had shared reports and talked over the phone about patients, we never met until one day when he visited his mother. As I fed Bea, he and his wife entered the room. There was an instant bond between us and we had a wonderful visit. As they left, we all hugged. It was a special moment.

Bea had a keen mind, quick wit and delightful sense of humor that she readily shared. During mealtime, we engaged in some upbeat conversations about family and friends as well as her beloved Packers where her loyalty was beyond reproach. Once during lunch, she expressed concern I might miss a meal. I told her not to worry for when it comes to food, I'm rarely shortchanged. Seldom have I seen a person in her condition so concerned about the welfare of others.

Bea liked to hear me sing the old songs. She would smile throughout the songfest and often sang along. She reported that some songs brought back childhood memories. For example, after we sang, "I'm Looking Over a Four Leaf Clover," she recalled, as a child crawling on her hands and knees in the yard as she looked for the treasures, and the excitement that occurred when she found one. Bea was such a neat lady and I treasured my time with her.

"Curt Kurt"

When I first met Kurt, he made an immediate impression. While upbeat and conversant, he had a sarcastic demeanor—not a mean one however. I am always leery to respond to sarcasm when I don't know whether intent is to reflect a negative attitude or to promote humor. In Kurt's case, I learned quickly it was humor and appreciated his quick wit. I intentionally left myself open for insults, and he capitalized with his best shots. He knew he could be himself around me and thrived on it. While I laughed at his barbs, he showed little emotion and maintained a sober look. Don Rickles would have been proud.

As an icebreaker, I asked Kurt what his profession was. He reported he was a mortician and owned a funeral home. Initially, I did not know whether to believe him, but later found this to be true. Obviously, I did not pursue any more discussions about it. I did proselytize about what a great place the residence was for those who required care. He responded, "Do I look cared for?" He caught me off-guard, and I was lost for words. I also asked how he liked the food and he answered, "I haven't gotten sick yet." In another food related incident, he requested a tossed salad made to order. When served a large portion, he commented, "You could feed seven rabbits with that stuff," and asked for a smaller helping.

Once when I greeted Kurt with my standard, "Happy Birthday," he looked confused. However, he quickly recalled the intent and commented how weird I was. When I saluted him for his good judgment, he quipped, "You are a character!" On another occasion, after he yawned several times, I asked if he was bored with the conversation. He responded quickly, "Actually yes." As I left, he got in another jab as he said, "Do something intelligent!" I continued my exit and tried to soothe a bruised ego.

Kurt did not think much of my singing. One day he observed me decked out in my quartet uniform and asked what the special occasion was. I told him we had a sing-out at an area high school that afternoon. He responded with another zinger, "What did they do to deserve that?"

When I learned Kurt loved sports and had been an athlete in high school, I told him of "Killer's" exploits on the gridiron and asked him, in a weak moment, if he was impressed. His two word response—"Actually not." That shut me up. When informed I graduated from The Ohio State University, he said, "What's your point?" Initially, I could not remember what it was, but then recalled it was the Buckeyes defeat at the hands of Southern California in a recent football game. He gave a semblance of a smile and said, "There is a God."

With reference to the Milwaukee Brewers baseball team, I asked who he thought would be the new manager, he quickly responded, "I'm busy." He inferred it might be a good job for me. When I inquired if he thought I would be a successful "skipper," he countered with an emphatic "No!"

In that it was a presidential election year, our conversations led to politics. While this violated one of my rules not to discuss controversial subjects with patients, I sensed Kurt had no loyalty to a particular party or candidate and felt we could have a fun conversation." When I asked for whom he was going to vote, he responded,

"I am going to write myself in again. You always vote for the best." There was no problem with self-image. He asked who my choice was. I told him I was going to write in Pat Paulson (a comedian from the past who, in jest, ran for president several times). He responded Pat died several years ago. I told him perhaps he could manage the country from heaven. Kurt had no response and "Killer" scored a rare point.

Once when I greeted Kurt, I observed him bleeding slightly from the face and neck. When asked what happened, he responded he cut himself while shaving and that the razor would be more effective to fillet fish. The next week, as I looked for a good quote, I asked if he had any more excruciating experiences to report. With pride and a sense of accomplishment, Kurt reported a blood free week.

One day when I told him about my book in progress entitled, *Hospice, Humor, Music and More: A Volunteer's Perspective*, he gave me a peculiar look and said, "Watch the use of colon!" That came from the punctuation mark in the title and maybe, in his case, referred to a body part.

Betsy in housekeeping, who frequently schemed to make me look bad, barged in one day when Kurt and I were engaged in a heavy conversation. She told him to press the emergency button if I bothered him. With a sadistic smile, he obliged. When staff arrived to handle the crisis, he proudly responded, "It only hurts for a little while and I'm over it." I was relieved.

Once I visited Kurt with a student nurse. As he observed a stethoscope, he said, "I see you're still wearing your first little doctor's set." She blushed and remained silent. As the conversation progressed, Kurt reported he knew her dad and they were members of the local Lions Club—what a small world. Rapport was quickly established and the young lady left with a fond memory of her late father thanks to Kurt. His type of humor had a positive impact on others—even me.

"Phil's Spirit and Caring for Family"

(Many hospice patients are in their senior years. They have lived rich, full lives and have a lifetime of memories to sustain them and their families. However, when people in the prime of life acquire terminal illness, life experiences end prematurely. They will not be around to watch their children grow into adulthood or realize dreams with family. Such is the case of Phil, diagnosed with terminal cancer at the age of 39. This sketch represents a warm, tender human-interest story of a dying man whose SELFLESS love for family consumes him to the end. The story, in many ways, parallels the life after illness of Randy Pausch with dedication to family. The "skunk story" highlights Phil's delightful sense of humor that he never lost.)

This vibrant young man had it all—a terrific wife, two beautiful children, a good job, many friends and a zest for life seldom seen. Family was Phil's number one priority. They were the love of his life.

Phil enlisted in the Air Force, was a veteran of the Gulf War and served his country in Desert Storm. He worked as a tool and dye repairman and was a part-time college student in pursuit of a degree. He enjoyed his Harley, restored old cars, woodworked and enjoyed sports, both as a participant and spectator. As are many, Phil was a huge Cubs' fan. In short, he was the all-American guy.

In his late 30s, Phil began to have health issues and subsequently had a series of medical tests. The initial diagnosis suggested he was cancer free and there was a good prognosis. However, shortly thereafter, his doctor returned, and with a sullen look, reported there was a mistake. The results were from another patient, and Phil's cancer was terminal. Although the news was a huge blow to Phil, just short of his 39th birthday, he recognized someone else had received positive news and was happy for them. He was not angry with the doctors for the mistaken diagnosis for he knew it would not change his fate. He forwent radiation treatment in favor of experimental drugs.

When I met Phil, he was in good spirits, had a positive outlook on life and willingly shared his story. He had a spiritual presence, was at peace and spent the final days doing things with and for family. Much like Randy Pausch, he did not focus on self but rather on his loved ones. It was all about them. Their future was everything to him. It was a heart-rending decision to leave them and spend his final days at the hospice residence. However, he and wife June did everything to keep the family together. She visited daily and the children (ages 8 and 10) came on a regular basis. To facilitate communication away from home, Phil utilized a webcam connected to a laptop computer.

With love and eager anticipation, Phil planned remembrances for June and the children. For June, he designed a special necklace that featured highlights of their life together (all too short), that he presented shortly before his death. He had mementos laid aside for his children. These included a perfect arrowhead, he discovered years before, for his daughter, and his favorite Chicago Cubs baseball hat for his son. He had three shadow boxes made that displayed honors and recognition of his military service, one for his wife and each child. He chose to give these and other items, accompanied by personalized notes, at future times. What a wonderful legacy!

Phil received terrific support from family. He had a devoted wife who did the special things. One day a framed autographed jersey of Donald Driver, star wide receiver of the Green Bay Packers, appeared in his room—a gift from June. With pride and the trace of a tear, he talked about the special gift and its significance.

Friends and others he had never met gave assistance. He showed pictures from a benefit fundraiser to help defray medical expenses. He also displayed a beautiful quilt made from 20 personalized patches, each from a different relative or friend. In spite of the goodness in people, Phil expressed disappointment that some friends no longer came around. Phil had a delightful sense of humor that he readily shared. His room was full of pictures of family, friends and experiences.

I observed a picture of a skunk on a bulletin board and asked about the story. He grinned and related how he and some friends in their youth came across three baby skunks as they crossed the street. Phil and his compatriots rescued the orphans and took them to a local restaurant, the boys' place of employment.

As a practical joke, they carefully placed the critters inside a five-gallon pail, marked it "ice bucket," and put a lid on top. They then hid with full view of the bucket and waited eagerly for someone to take the bait. When an unsuspecting employee opened the bucket, a scream echoed down the street, and there was the chaos they had eagerly anticipated.

I asked Phil if these youngsters had developed their "stinking mechanisms." He replied that they had but were not yet fully developed. Therefore, there was a stink but a tolerable one—at least for a short period of time. The mounted picture of the skunk was from Phil's father-in-law, a not so subtle reminder of a fun memory.

When I talked with June at Phil's funeral visitation, she reminded her daughter of the Cubs' baseball (with a panoramic view of Wrigley Field) I gave him to honor his beloved team. He had passed this treasure on to his daughter. I felt blessed. In spite of a life that ended prematurely, Phil's legacy is intact.

"Tribute to Cheryl"

(This case illustrates the importance of support for family as a loved one nears death. When volunteers or friends are present at this mournful time, it reassures family that they're not alone and people care.)

When introduced to Cheryl, she was comatose. At bedside were her husband Tom, and soul mate of 52 years, a daughter, daughter-in-law and two grandchildren. I listened as the family spoke about how special she was and the positive impact she had on others. As they admired pictures in family albums, they shared remembrances and testimonies of their loved one.

Cheryl, adored by family and friends, was gregarious by nature, a "social butterfly," and the life of the party. She made things happen and got everyone involved. Her extraordinary smile and exemplary people skills brought out the best in all. With a quick wit and delightful sense of humor, she made people laugh and kept them entertained. Talent abounded. She was an accomplished artist, an excellent dancer, a polished actress and an enthusiastic songster. As a member of The Red Hat Society, she had a forum to highlight her talents.

In retirement years, Tom and Cheryl spent winter months in Florida where their social life challenged those half their age. They were risk-takers and often shared "youthful" experiences with grandchildren. They danced (clogging being their specialty), biked, went white river rafting and even bungee jumped. To no one's surprise, Cheryl organized fun things for the geriatric jet set. One of her first ventures was to organize a kitchen band that featured talented musicians who played such classic in-struments as kazoos, drums, pie pans and washboards. Music piped from heaven. You had to be there. This form of entertainment was so successful that it expanded to a variety show (now named in her honor) that Cheryl or-ganized and directed.

Cheryl fought the illness and maintained a sense of humor to the end. When her doctor asked if the pre-scribed narcotics caused discomfort, she turned her head, squinted her eyes, stuck out her tongue and sneered. Her feisty spirit prevailed. In another instance, the nurse pulled sheets to shift her position in bed. When asked if comfortable, she smiled, looked up and pointed her fin-ger upward—a celestial moment. Before Cheryl lost con-sciousness, she gazed lovingly at Tom and said, "The best part of me is you." What a wonderful way to say goodbye.

Cheryl's family, when they learned of my interest in the old songs, requested I sing a few of her favorites. As she lay in a comatose state, I grasped her hand and sang a number of the "oldies." During the musical interlude, the family gazed fondly at their loved one as they observed subtle behavioral responses. These included changes in handgrip, an anticipatory smile, slight eye movements and altered respiration. Tearfully, they expressed gratitude for the special moment. Before I left, we all hugged.

Cheryl's grandchildren reflected what she meant to them. In the tribute, they give their impressions for each letter of her first and last names. The comments reveal lots about this marvelous lady, what made her tick and how adored she was by her family. The reflections that related to humor are in bold. To protect Cheryl's identity, the letters are out of sequence.

"What You Mean to Us"
A Tribute from Cheryl's Grandchildren

A   "Amazing artist—Just look at the beautiful paintings in her house—Wow!"
    "Able to make light of any moment, no matter how difficult."
    "Admired for your positive and loving personality."
    "Always the gracious host."

C   "Classy, yet sassy."
    "Can't hold back from a good party."

"Celebrated a long life of adventure, happiness and unforgettable memories."
"Continuous comedian."

J "Jovial Jokester."
"Jolly and playful spirit."
"Just a joy to be around."

O "Oath taken to love Tom forever and ever."
"Opportunity knocks, you answer."
"Occupation—Social Director."
"Oozes with warm-hearted sarcasm."

R "Rower—Just recently competed in a rowing contest with Tom."
"Ready to play any type of game day or night."
"Refined sense of style."
"Rowdy sense of humor."

A "Actively involved in making everyday count and worthwhile."
"Accomplished many goals and dreams in your life."
"Animated."
"Always will be in our hearts."

B "Busy...always up to something, aren't you?"
"Beautiful lady inside and out."
"Blah, blah, blah."

"Blessed with wonderful family and friends that think the world of you."

C "Children—Mark, Donna, and Denise are so blessed to have you for their mom."
"Celebrated in style 50 years of blissful marriage to Tom—What a party that was!"
"Creative painter and costume maker."
"Courageously battling a sudden illness."

I "Infectious, happy spirit."
"Invaluable part of so many peoples' lives."
"It could not have happened to a nicer person and much too soon."
"Is going to be loved and remembered warmly long after you are beamed up to heaven."

L **"Loves to laugh and make other people laugh."**
"Lived in Florida for a while."
"Life—Always full of it."
"Loves to spend quality time with family and friends."

O "Original, no fillers!"
"Oh crap—Why does this have to happen?"
"Outgoing."
"Outstanding positive outlook on life no matter what God throws at you."

Although Cheryl never uttered a word, as I left that day, I felt I knew her and was blessed.

"Merle's Special Talent"

While Merle had a developmental disability, he was able to care for himself before illness. He never married and his only family was a sister he had not seen in years. He was a quiet man and a loner. He had few friends and seldom a visitor. He displayed little emotion and rarely smiled. While communication skills were adequate to carry on simple conversations, he had few interests and to carry on a substantive conversation was a challenge. He spent most of his day with eyes glued to the television. He was easy to care for and never bothered anyone. Socially, Merle was a person that "passed through the cracks." Yet, he survived with little help and made the most with what he had. He was the person you wanted to befriend but didn't know how to do so. I wondered how often this lonely man experienced fun times in his lifetime.

Initially, I was not able to reach or connect with Merle. However, one day a sudden change occurred. As I took him for a walk around the grounds, I started to sing whatever came to mind. There was a transformation in Merle's demeanor and he started to sing along. He actually remembered more of the words and sang fewer "la la's" than I did. As I listened with interest, I wondered why it took so long to thrust my music on him. I did with everyone else. Somewhere in his earlier years, music was a part of his life. It just took me longer to get it out of him.

After our walk, we resumed the sing-along in the living room. Soon we had an audience, and Merle was in his element. For the first time, I saw a smile and it looked good on him. Much like Maude ("Maude's Selective Memory"), he got a kick out of singing words that I intentionally omitted. There was humor. For the first time, Merle was in charge. When I took him back to his room, he grasped my hand, smiled and requested I return next week. I accepted the invitation. This reinforced the power of music as a communicator that can work with people at all levels of functioning.

When I returned, Merle greeted me with a smile and asked if we were going to sing again. He was ready and so was I. We quickly got into our songfest and went through the repertoire. As we sang, Merle looked surprised and said, "You know all the songs I know." I smiled for as we sang, there was a slight delay (barely noticeable) from my lyrics to his.

Fortunately, when I sang with Merle, I had my book of lyrics that did wonders for both our memories. During our songfests, Merle had the time of his life, would sometimes giggle out-of-the-blue and show a rare display of emotion. He never tired as he sang the old songs and loved to share his vocals with others. Special times occurred when someone paid attention to him. The hospice staff was good at that.

There was a spiritual side to Merle. One day he requested we take a walk in subfreezing temperatures. As we double-timed to expedite circulation, he began to sing, "Jesus Loves Me." I think he thought God was closer outdoors. Soon after, I joined in. To my surprise, I felt an inner peace and spiritual presence. As our relationship grew, so did the firmness of his handshake. We had a real connection.

"Tommy the Drummer"

When I introduced myself to Tommy and his family, I learned we had some mutual friends. This was a great icebreaker and rapport was quickly established.

Our conversation turned to music that brought a smile to Tommy. He had been a professional drummer, and had played with the Ron Harvey orchestra, a local group with a national reputation. This gave me a perfect opportunity to perform an instrumental from the big band era. I positioned my hand trumpet, took a deep breath and quickly played my renditions of Russ Morgan's, "Does Your Heart Beat for Me," followed by Clyde McCoy's, "Sugar Blues," much like I did for Ivan ("Ivan and the Big Bands"). While I played, Tommy was all smiles as he waved hands and arms passionately to simulate drum movements. While I played, I closed my eyes and imagined drumbeats in precise rhythm to the sound from the trumpet. Unfortunately, I never saw Tommy again for he died before I returned. However, I enjoyed our short time together. There was chemistry and an instant bond.

After Tommy's death, I fantasized about a celestial band—Ivan on the fiddle ("Ivan and the Big Bands"), Marty on the trumpet ("Marty the Consummate Musician") and Tommy on the drums. I even included myself (big surprise) as a backup for Marty and as a performer with the one-man-band if the occasion warranted. In any case, I bet those three are playing great music with the big band in the sky.

"Joel's Miracle"

(I always encourage hope for hospice patients; a pleasant thought that looks to the future. For many, it's the last thing they have to hold on to. Even as death approaches, hope abounds for those faithful who anticipate a better life to follow. On a rare occasion, a patient outlives the hospice placement and a miracle occurs that supports the adage, "As long as there's life, there's hope." Such was the case with Joe whose story is described below.)

One day at the Home, a gentleman greeted me with a hug and cheery "Happy Birthday Jack," and asked if I remembered him. Truthfully, I didn't as evidenced by my blank expression—a fairly typical occurrence. Through the years, I've had contacts with numerous hospice patients and as I frequently say, "While I have a good memory, it's short." Joel's time there preceded work on the book and before I took notes of patient visits.

Joel bailed me out as he introduced himself and gave background information. In his early 50s he had a terminal illness, so he thought. As I came out of the fog with memory refreshed somewhat, we reminisced about our time together. I recalled his gregarious personality and good people skills as well as his passion for music. He was an accomplished musician and had his own band.

When a patient, Joel's physical appearance reflected serious illness. Now he looked entirely different. With a new lease on life, he was the picture of health and again played in the band. What a wonderful moment to see the transformation—truly a miracle. Joel was now a volunteer as he gave back the emotional support he received. What a perfect role for he'd been there.

"Franz and the Kids"

Franz had a German dialect that fit his heritage. After many years as a farmer, he became a school custodian where he was a friend and confidant to many students. He was a "people person," a good conversationalist and compassionate listener. The students thought enough of him to dedicate a school year book in his honor. He was a special person and a role model.

Franz was yet another patient who enjoyed the old songs. As I sang, he mouthed the words and, with his hands, beat time to the music. The "golden oldies" resurrected memories from bygone days. Maybe he flew on the trapeze, took a sentimental journey, rode a bicycle built for two, cruised down the river or sailed on moonlight bay.

Once when I sang, he started to doze. As I observed his lethargic state, I asked if my songs made him drowsy. He responded, "No—I'm thinking." Perhaps, It was a time to reminisce. In any case, he was contented and relaxed.

Jill, a hospice nurse, has a delightful sense of humor that she readily shares with patients. She's been known to break out in a song or throw out a one-liner or two as she cares for patients. Once when Jill attended to Franz, for whatever reason (not that she needed one), she started to recite the nursery rhyme, "Simple Simon met a pie man." Before she could go further, Franz interrupted, revealed his jovial side and suggested an additive to the pie that was not edible. Although Franz's comment was a bit on the risqué side, Jill was pleased with his sense of humor and so was I.

I only saw Franz two more times before his death and regret that I did not know him better. He truly made a difference and touched the lives of many.

"Stan and the Missing Parts"

I first met Stan when I fed him breakfast. Not surprisingly, I sensed frustration on his part for loss of independence. However, he perked up when he talked about family—a wife of 57 years, five children and nine grandchildren.

It didn't take long to discover Stan's snappy sense of humor. Much like Kurt ("Curt Kurt"), his responses to questions were terse but funny. Before breakfast, I inquired if he was hungry. He gave me a look of disbelief and insinuated he couldn't be hungry if he didn't have his teeth. The problem was quickly rectified, and he again was able to chew. Fortunately, he made it through the morning meal with little help on my part. While humor was his intent, he maintained a sober look and never cracked a smile. When asked if he was from Milwaukee, he quickly responded, "Most of the time." I laughed.

Stan asked what other things I did to occupy time in retirement. I gave him my standard answer, "To drive my wife crazy." That opened the door for another terse comment as he responded, "I can understand why." I told him my wife and I spend a couple of months as "Winter Texans" on South Padre Island that is close to the Mexican border. When Stan asked if there were any problems traveling to and from Mexico, I gave him straight answers and followed with an embarrassing moment that occurred on our way home several years ago.

The border patrol guard asked if we were United State's citizens. Without hesitation, I responded, "No, we're from Wisconsin." I wasn't trying to be flippant and have no idea why I responded that way. I do know the border guard wasn't amused (neither was my wife) and, in disgust, waved us through. It's now standard policy for my wife to do all talking when we make this required stop. As I finished the description of the incident, Stan gave me his standard look of disbelief and shook his head. While I didn't achieve my goal to elicit a smile, I sensed he enjoyed the moment.

Stan's wife and a daughter gave more background information about the man they adored. Through the years, he held a number of jobs that displayed a versatility of skills. He worked on the railroad and did some farming and carpentry work. He came from a family of musicians and played the harmonica and button accordion. He liked to have fun and was a good storyteller.

Stan and his wife loved to dance and were in their element when they did the polka. This gave me the perfect opportunity to do my rendition of the classic polka, "Just Because." It was my hope to get Stan's seal of approval, but such wasn't the case. He glared at me and said nothing.

I remained unflappable and started to sing, "Beer Barrel Polka." Hardly into the song, Stan stopped me and offered his critique. Not so subtly, he responded, "You're way off!" In a state of shock, I ended the song prematurely and tried to figure my next move. While I wasn't certain whether he was serious, I gave him the benefit of the doubt and went home to practice. However, I never had the courage to try a repeat performance. One rejection was enough.

Stan put things in perspective and maintained a sense of humor throughout his illness. This showed in his favorite t-shirt monogrammed with the words, "Parts Missing." As one might conclude, the missing parts resulted from a number of surgeries. They all began with the letter /p/—personal, private and practical. I didn't pursue what the missing parts were. I can only speculate.

"Rita the Polka Queen"

My visits with Rita were memorable. She was an adorable lady with a pleasant demeanor and a captivating smile. The happy look never left her face nor did the sparkle in her eyes. While no longer able to speak, she comprehended and loved to be included in conversations. Two daughters talked lovingly about their mother and her ability to bring out the best in people. They mused over her delightful sense of humor and love of practical jokes. They chuckled as they recalled a couple of humorous instances.

As a prankster, Rita created a "haunted room" at work to initiate new employees. Eerie sounds and visual effects brought fear to even the strongest of heart, and screams were the norm—Halloween all year round. However, most workers recovered from the prank and lived to work another day. In another instance, Rita made a friend a sponge cake out of real sponges and finished it off with a delectable icing. It was quite a site as her friend sampled the icing and then attempted to cut the cake—a memorable birthday to say the least.

Rita loved to polka and in her senior years could still out strut people half her age. Much like Cheryl ("Cheryl's Legacy"), she was skilled at getting the timid to dance and wanted everyone to have fun. She was a polka groupie and followed area bands around the circuit. I could just imagine Rita as she danced with a wide array of partners, all thrilled to polka with the best.

With this background, I considered Rita a good risk for a songfest and wasn't disappointed. When I sang the two polka songs that I know and overuse ("Beer Barrel Polka" and "Just Because"), she took on another life as she waved her arms, moved her legs and tapped her feet to the rhythm of the music. In fact, she was so into the music, I feared she might fall out of bed. Fortunately, she didn't. Rita's reaction to my polka songs was in sharp contrast to that of Stan's ("Stan and the Missing Parts") and went a long way to repair a bruised ego.

Next, I sang some of the classics that only a person in Rita's age group would appreciate: "I'm Looking Over a

Four Leaf Clover," "Toot, Toot, Tootsie," "Wait Till the Sun Shines Nellie," "You are My Sunshine," "When You Wore a Tulip," "Five Foot Two, Eyes of Blue," "If You Knew Suzie," "I Want a Girl," and many others. She was thrilled and, with her signature smile, made happy vocalizations. It was obvious the music brought back pleasant memories. It was fun to guess what they were.

"Fun with Charlie the Canine"

(A support system addressing psychological and spiritual needs is an important component of hospice care. The story below involves a spouse of a hospice patient, her love for animals and visits from a dog (unofficial as they were) that brought some happy moments.)

Animals often bring happiness and contentment to those with illness. Tom often took his docile yellow lab, Charlie, to visit his mother Stella. Charlie not only brought Stella pleasure but, in the true spirit of hospice, did the same for other patients and families as well. Millie, the wife of another patient, spent 24/7 at her husband's side and was in need of respite. So when Stella received visits from Charlie, it was the perfect opportunity for Millie, a dog lover, to greet her friend. Little did Stella know that she was not the primary recipient. Eventually she got the picture and accepted the role of "second fiddle" to a canine.

Whenever Millie entered the room, Charlie, with tail wagging, would make a mad dash in her direction. He knew top priority treatment was about to occur. Millie, oblivious to Stella's presence, would greet her canine friend with a smile and say all the right things to feed his ego. As she petted, tickled and gave him special treats, Charlie was in "doggy heaven."

A real bond ensued between Millie and Charlie. Tom also enjoyed these light moments as did Stella whose friendship with Millie became even stronger. However, for the record, Charlie never wanted to leave and relished the special attention he received from a newfound friend.

"Vera's Celestial Smile"

My first visit with Vera was a memorable one. Present were Fred, her soul mate of 58 years, and their two daughters. While no longer able to speak because of a stroke, she understood and enjoyed conversations. She displayed a radiant smile that filled the room with good will and her eyes, "the window of her soul," had that spark and warmth only good people have.

Later in the day, there was a Christmas celebration. Even Santa, who looked vaguely familiar, and an elf, who resembled a daughter of Vera's, were there. Children and grandchildren of staff personally delivered their requests to the jolly old guy while they sat on his lap. As Vera nodded her head in approval, she took in all of the festivities and displayed her signature smile. The fun songs, "Rudolph the Red Nose Reindeer," and "Jingle Bells," followed by the hymns, "Silent Night," and "Joy to the World," really got her into the spirit of the season.

The next week when I entered her room, she smiled and had the signature twinkle in her eye. I grasped her hand and began to sing "When You're Smiling." As the song progressed, she tightened her grip and excitedly mouthed the words. When I finished the number, Vera's daughters expressed their appreciation and requested that I sing more songs. Not accustomed to compliments, I volunteered to sing my entire repertoire. However, I offered a disclaimer and confessed, while I can remember melodies of songs, I have problems with words. Therefore, I had to refer to my book of lyrics—as I do with many patients. The modification did not seem to bother Vera or her family.

That day the adrenalin flowed, and as I got more into the music, my voice became louder. As the sound rattled the rafters, there was a light tap at the door. Sister Vivian, a dear lady in her 80s with a gentle demeanor, appeared. Consistent with her role as a hospice volunteer, she politely asked if I would sing more softly. While I am pretty much an all-or-nothing singer, I tried to comply with Sister's request. When she did not return, I assumed I was in compliance.

When I came back from a two-month winter vacation, I was pleased to know that Vera was still a patient, and I was eager to see her. As soon as she saw me, that amazing smile reappeared and there was immediate recognition. It was déjà vu as I proceeded to sing every "oldie" that I knew and a few others where I made up the words. Vera maintained that radiant smile throughout the songfest that lasted over an hour. While confined to bed, she still would beat out the time of the songs with her feet. You could tell when a song renewed memories of the past; she became excited and tried to sing along. I shared this special experience with Fred and her son. Vera died before I returned the next week. I thought the special time we had together the week before might have been her way to say goodbye.

"Gloria's Affectionate Kicks"

Gloria, a dear lady, with a strong will and feisty spirit was one of my first patients. I think she sensed my neophyte status and took advantage of it. She was in the latter stages of ALS and no longer able to speak. We had difficulty with communication. When she mouthed words without voice, I comprehended segments through lipreading, but meaning was lost.

We did communicate some nonverbally using a magic slate and notepad. However, we both lacked penmanship. When we did communicate, delays occurred and spontaneity was lost. To promote comprehension, I would initiate conversation and ask questions to elicit "Yes" or "No" responses. While not foolproof, it helped reestablish a connection.

Gloria and I developed excellent rapport. She had a fun side and loved to tease me. While a grin was difficult to distinguish from a sneer, I generally knew when she was in a good mood and when I treaded on thin ice. She could still move her feet and legs and made the most of the motor activity. One of Gloria's most effective forms of nonverbal communication was the use of a kick. She received great pleasure when she kicked me in the legs. Being a masochist, I always made certain to be in the line of fire. She had a variety of kicks I could identify. A strong kick meant she was angry; a weak kick suggested she was pleased; and the absence of a kick showed disinterest in the conversation. Gloria liked a good joke or story and tolerated some of my singing. I so looked forward to the mild kicks for I wanted to please her and welcomed fewer bruises to my legs.

Gloria never thought her illness was terminal and was determined to beat it. She had eternal hope. Even in the advanced stages of disease, she felt a cure was close and was always prepared to return home. With bags packed, she was ready for a quick exit. Little did Gloria know it was for a heavenly home—or did she?

"Escapades with Dudley and the Power Chair"

(One of the most valued freedoms is the ability to move about without assistance. Generally, one gives the privilege little thought and takes it for granted. When illness takes away this ability, there is a sudden disruption of life's function and a loss of independence. People become devastated, as they have to rely on others to satisfy basic needs. Such was the case with Dudley. When given the opportunity to move about again independently with a power chair, he enjoyed the freedom but could not operate the machine safely.)

When health issues forced Dudley to surrender his driver's license, he was devastated. The final blow occurred when he no longer could walk without assistance. When confined to a wheelchair, Dudley became morose and depressed. However, when trained to use an electric chair (not a good choice of words), let's say power chair, he acquired a new lease on life, at least temporarily.

It didn't take Dudley much time to gain attention from hospice staff. While he ordinarily had a meek and mild disposition, he took on a different personality as he navigated his new toy. He loved the independence as he was again in control. Unfortunately, he exhibited less than exemplary driving skills.

People feared for their lives as Dudley drove his power chair full speed ahead without regard for the safety of pedestrians. When asked to slow down and be more considerate of people in the line of fire, Dudley refused. As he began his ride, staff would use their walky-talkies to warn everyone to take cover. He took sadistic pleasure to see how close he could come to someone and still avoid a collision.

As Dudley cruised outside, he negotiated hairline turns around the ground's labyrinth without a hitch and avoided a plunge into the pond. Miraculously, he never had an accident. Staff and volunteers took solace in that they knew some bigger power looked down on Dudley and relished the moments when he was happy and in his element. However, they soon realized that an accident was inevitable and took away his treasured vehicle.

As expected, Dudley was again devastated with the loss of independence. He didn't take the loss lightly and schemed how he could get the power chair back. Bribery seemed a reasonable way to go. With a slight grin, he offered $100 to anyone who would get the chair out of storage and return it to its rightful owner. Dudley had no takers, and his driving days were over. However, in the days ahead, with support from staff, he was able to regain the ability to smile and make the most out of his remaining days.

"Songs and Stories with Vivian"

When I first saw Vivian, she greeted me with a hearty smile and a firm handshake. She made me feel welcome and I hope I did her as well. There was instant compatibility and conversation flowed. She talked with affection of her husband of 60 years. She was 17 and he 19 when they married. Some thought the marriage would not last past the teen years. As the happy couple defied odds, Vivian's mother remarked they were luckier than smart, not a huge vote of confidence. In any case, the pair had a loving relationship and warm family life.

I thought Vivian would be a good candidate for a song or two and was not disappointed. Vivian thought I had a great voice and who was I to disagree. I could do no wrong. Many of the tunes brought back old memories. After I sang, "Let the Rest of the World Go By," Vivian, with a look of surprise and warm smile, said, "How did you know that was our favorite song?" I quickly responded, "Lucky I guess." I continued my streak of clairvoyance when I did "Side by Side," a number sung at her wedding.

Vivian expressed an interest in my family and asked about my wife. In jest, I told her, while married for 49 years, we've only had five good years together and not consecutive either. That statement brought a puzzled look and a delayed smile. In that she knew the "golden oldies" played a significant role in my life, she asked what song my wife and I enjoyed the most? Without hesitation, I replied, "I Got Along Without You before I Met You; I'll get Along without You Now." The response caught Vivian off-guard, but she recovered and quickly stated my wife must be a saint to have put up with me all these years. (I've heard that a few times before.) When she asked if my wife worked, I told her she had a full time job taking care of me. She promptly responded, "I can understand why." Vivian liked to pick on me, not that I gave her any opportunities. I was pleased.

Vivian had my number and I enjoyed every minute for the frivolity brought laughter. She had some great one-liners. When I asked if she would like a bird feeder outside her window, she responded, "I like birds to fly around, but don't need a crowd in the window." Once when I asked Vivian how she felt, she answered, "I'm kicking but not so high." In another instance (for some reason), there was conversation relative to housework. My volunteer cohort asked if I ever dusted. Vivian quickly responded, "He probably does—drags his feet across the floor." I loved her quick wit and sense of humor.

"Divine Intervention with Seth"

(Sometimes incidents occur with hospice patients that have no worldly explanation. They are of a spiritual nature and suggest divine intervention. Such is the experience with Seth.)

When I met Seth, he was bedridden and in the advanced stage of illness. He and his wife had spent their adult lives as missionaries in Japan. This man of God had a kind look and compassionate demeanor that fit his profession. He was so appreciative of the care he received and ready to meet his maker.

Seth's communication skills were severely impaired. While he spoke primarily in jargon and had few intelligible utterances, he comprehended speech when given ample time to process what he heard. Nonverbal communication consisted of head nods, eye movements and hand gestures.

The last time I saw Seth, he was in a semi-comatose state, restless and in some discomfort. However, there were periods of lucidity. As I sat by his bedside, I stroked his hand and felt the need to stay. As I searched for words of comfort, I asked if he would like me to read from the Bible. He nodded in approval. I picked up the Gideon Bible from his bed stand. While I didn't know what passage might be appropriate, I arbitrarily decided on a Psalm. As I opened the Book, Psalm 103 appeared.

When I began to read, "Bless the Lord, O my soul; and all that is within me, bless his holy name," a remarkable transformation took place. Seth smiled, grasped my hand and was at instant peace. As I read, he began to mouth the scripture. He knew it well. The more I read the more I realized I could not have selected a more appropriate passage. From verses 15-17, "As for man, his days are like grass; he flourishes like a flower of the field; for the wind passes over it and it is gone, and its place knows it no more. But the steadfast love of the Lord is from everlasting to everlasting upon those who fear him and his righteousness to children's children." Verse 19—"The Lord has established his throne in the heavens and his kingdom rules over all."

Later I learned Psalm 103 was one of Seth's favorite scriptures for those about to take the celestial journey. What a coincidence I thought. There are 150 Psalms in the Bible and fortuitously Psalm 103 emerged. I related this experience to Sister Sue who indicated God directed me to read that passage and called it divine intervention. I believe that. Seth died that evening. This experience strengthened my faith. I felt privileged and blessed to have been a part of this spiritual encounter.

"Helen's Impact"

(Sometimes hospice volunteers are the first to comfort and support family and friends after the death of their loved one. At this critical time, they are in need of caring and compassion from others. Hugs abound and warm remembrances are shared.)

One day Sister Sue requested I give support to the family and friends of Helen who died an hour before. As I entered Helen's room, I observed about a dozen people at her side. I introduced myself and learned that most were part of her inner sanctum. As they grasped hands, they shared memories about their dear friend. I soon realized the monumental impact Helen had on the lives of so many.

I learned that Helen was selfless and always gave to others. She looked for the best in people and situations and had a signature smile that was a permanent fixture. While she had a diverse group of friends from all backgrounds and lifestyles, she possessed the unique ability to get personalities to mesh and for everyone to interact effectively. She was the organizer, social director and the life of the party. She made things go and was always there for her pals.

After Helen's compatriots shared cathartic experiences about their departed friend, they requested I read scripture. In Sister Sue's absence, I shared my spiritual incident with Seth ("Divine Intervention with Seth") and the significance of Psalm 103. Once again, I read the passage as they tearfully listened. When finished, I gave each a hug, stroked the arm of Helen as she lay in repose with rosary in hand and quietly left the room. I pictured this remarkable woman when active and healthy and felt confident I could have picked her out of a group.

"Mel's Celebration of Life"

For about 15 years, Mel battled a chronic pulmonary disorder, which left him with respiratory difficulties and a number of other ailments. In spite of failing health, he remained good-natured and openly talked about his condition.

While confined to a wheelchair, Mel enjoyed the walks we took around the picturesque grounds. He relaxed in a patio area that overlooked a pond and several acres of prairie and woods. He loved the out-of-doors and became excited as he observed the wonders of nature. He watched a doe and her two fawns as they roamed in the prairie, gazed at a majestic egret as it waded in the pond and admired a swallow as it circled the water and swooped down to catch an elusive water bug. He observed the antics of a gopher as it explored the grounds, listened to the deep croak of a bullfrog, watched the cattails blow in the breeze and looked for fish movement in the pond. Mel related when he planted some fish in the Home's pond from a number of catches several years before and wondered if any survived.

When Mel ate in the kitchen, he gazed out the window to look at the landscape. He could spot a red tailed hawk perched on a tree from a hundred yards or a turkey in a distant cornfield. He loved to share his discoveries with staff and offered binoculars to confirm his findings. One day as Mel took in all the beauty, he looked at me reflectively and said, "This is a good place to die."

Mel, as an outdoorsman, liked to hunt and fish. As a fisherman, he knew all the hot spots and even made his own lures. He caught many trophy fish and always liked to share his expertise with others—me included. As an avid fisherman, Mel stated metaphorically, "The Lord keeps throwing me back as a sheepshead." (*In Wisconsin lakes, the sheepshead is a scavenger fish that doesn't appear on the plates of many Friday fish fries; anglers generally release these undesirables for someone else to catch. Much like Mel, they were survivors and kept coming back.*)

In the several months Mel was a patient, we engaged in many cordial conversations, some serious and others on the light side. He maintained a positive outlook on life and made every day count. He had a great sense of humor and was gregarious by nature. He had a quick wit that he used generously. Once when I did a lead-in, "You know what I heard," he interrupted "Sheep!" In another instance, when we greeted each other with my standard "Happy Birthday," Mel expressed merriment that we shared the same special day although his was in December and mine in April. He followed with a memorable quote, "We are brothers; we just have different mothers." We were brothers, and I loved him dearly.

Once when Mel requested my presence, Katie, another volunteer, appeared. He quickly stated, "You're not Jack." Being a quick wit Katie responded, "Happy Birthday—Now am I Jack?" What fun this "birthday thing" is.

One morning after he read the local newspaper, Mel gazed at me and, with a grin, said it was going to be a good day. When I asked why? He replied he didn't see his name in the obituary section. Another time he grinned and said, "I woke up this morning with nothing to do and at the end of the day only had it half-done." What a great sense of humor he had.

Mel loved practical jokes, and illness did not prevent him from being a participant in their planning. Betsy, of the housekeeping staff (frequently mentioned in this book), kept the place tidy and frequently wet-mopped the kitchen floor. She made certain people remained "a foot" as they entered the room, and strategically placed "Wet Floor" signs.

When these barriers occurred around lunchtime, Mel encountered difficulty as he entered the kitchen. Once in an attempt to solve the problem, he consulted with Gladys, a staff nurse to devise a scheme. She confiscated the signboards (after the drying process) and transported them to his room for display. When Betsy learned of the theft and confronted Mel, he pleaded ignorance. However, as a spiritual person, he speculated it might have been divine intervention. He did report that he liked the new decorations that adorned the walls of his room. Betsy was not a "happy camper," quickly removed the signboards, and abruptly left the room. Other people, unknown to me, hid Betsy's housekeeping cart and unplugged the cord to her vacuum cleaner.

I said goodbye to Mel before I left for vacation and questioned whether I'd ever see him again. Before I left, he gave me a silver dollar and a big hug, unusual behavior for a person so frugal and not prone to outward displays of affection. I thought at the time it might be his way to say goodbye, and it was. While I fell one week short to share in his "Celebration of Life," his memory lives on as I recall the remarkable times we had together. Because of Mel, I have a greater love and respect for the beauty of nature and never miss an opportunity to search for a red tailed hawk.

"Dining with Verona"

The cooks do a terrific job in preparing meals that generally please even the most critical of palates. However, with illness, comes the loss of appetite and taste ("Betty and the Hamburgers"). Others love everything they eat ("Everything is Wonderful Harry," and "Dear Lady from England"). They feed the cooks' egos and encourage their culinary resourcefulness. Verona loved to eat, and there weren't many food items she didn't enjoy.

I met Verona when she had breakfast. When I introduced myself as "Jack," she grinned and responded with a segment from a fairy tale, "Jack in the beanstalk looking for a golden goose." I liked her style. For a lady so small in stature, Verona could really put it away. While she didn't utter a word, I sat in amazement as she consumed a large bowl of cereal topped with sliced bananas. Next, she polished off a large helping of scrambled eggs, a couple strips of bacon and two pieces of toast topped with peanut butter. In between bites, she sipped on a large glass of cranberry juice and then tackled another. Not finished, she consumed three homemade chocolate chip cookies. When I asked Verona if she enjoyed breakfast, she responded in the affirmative and reported her appetite had just started to return. Wow! I thought how much did she eat before?

After breakfast, Verona and I engaged in conversation that, of course, led to song. After I sang "When You're Smiling," (big surprise) in the best voice I could muster, I asked if she would like to hear another number. She gave me a stern look and quickly replied, "No!' Not wishing to sing to unsympathetic ears, I complied with her wish.

As I recognized this feisty lady had a good sense of humor, I told her a few of my favorite stories. She followed with one of her best. In the middle of the tale, she stopped abruptly and whispered in my ear, "I can't finish; Sister is here." Sister Katrina encouraged Verona to continue for there wasn't much she hadn't heard before. In that Verona didn't resume the story, I assumed the material was not for public consumption, at least for those that wore the habit.

I excused myself and left the dining room while I took another patient for a walk around the grounds. Our time outside came to an abrupt end when I sat on a wet lawn chair. With a soaked posterior, I returned to the dining room and complained about my condition. Verona observed the damage and unsympathetically stated, "That little wetness in your pants isn't going to hurt anything." This spunky lady, who I had met an hour before, put me in my place, and I was lost for words—a rarity. About two hours after breakfast, Verona returned to her room for a nap before lunch.

While I only saw Verona on two occasions, she left an impression. She never talked about her health issues and maintained a positive outlook on life. There was a warm, kind side to her that she readily shared. To another volunteer she said, "Your heart is as sunny as your hair," and to me, "You're a good person; you can see it in your eyes."

"Happy Jordy and His Love for Life"

Jordy, at age 91, had a zest for life seldom seen in people half his age. He was still grateful for life, even as compromised as it was. My first visit with him was a memorable one. He greeted me with a pleasant hello and a warm smile. When I introduced myself as a volunteer, he responded, "That's nice Jack. I'm glad you're here." I didn't expect such a warm response and felt an instant bond. Some individuals look for the best in people and situations and always seem happy and contented. They adhere to the adage, "If you can't say something nice, don't say anything at all." You feel good in their presence. Jordy was such a person. Even as health deteriorated, his mood never changed, and he remained grateful for the fellowship.

I told Jordy I was a singer (of sorts) and asked if he'd like to hear a few songs. Not surprisingly, he said, "Yes." I sensed he would like a songfest and be a receptive audience and wasn't disappointed. "When You're Smiling," fit his personality to a tee and he smiled throughout. Afterwards, he commented on what a nice voice I had. As I craved the positive reinforcement, I went through my entire repertoire of "golden oldies." It was such a treat to see Jordy so content and responsive to the music. Sometimes, Katie, my volunteer friend, would display her considerable vocal talents and join me in a duet. Whether we sang a hymn or an old song, Jordy enjoyed the harmony. With a smile, he would nod his head to the rhythm of the music.

Both Jordy and I looked forward to our weekly songfests that were better when Katie joined us. As he memorized lyrics, he would simultaneously break out in smile and song, and sometimes a trio ensued. Jordy chuckled when we told him we ought to take our trio on tour, but only if the price was right. We all had fun together.

Jordy had a good sense of humor and enjoyed a good story. Once when I talked about the winter weather with generous amounts of the white stuff, I told him I had a long driveway with lots of snow to shovel. I followed that I got my wife a snow shovel for Christmas and reported how adept she was at the task. He smiled, shook his head and said, "I know you're kidding. You're too nice of guy to have her shovel snow." I really had him fooled.

My comedy never got a better reception than it did from Jordy. Even the marginal material brought laughter. His laugh was one of the best I ever heard and was entertainment in and by itself. He put his heart and soul into laughter. It was loud, coarse and occurred without restraints—the guffaw type. It was music to my ears.

I often shared humor with Jordy from performances by my barbershop quartets. I have a two-line poem that I recite in all seriousness and milk it for everything I can get. It goes, *"Yellow banana so sweet and fair; have I the right to strip you bare?"* He laughed and said the poem was short but good and that I was a funny guy. I accepted that.

I then related how a friend of mine in his retirement years discovered he had talent for painting portraits. Subsequently, he put an ad in the local newspaper that advertised his work. Several days later, he received a call from a lady who wished to have her picture painted in the nude. He was a bit embarrassed and told her he didn't paint those kinds of pictures. She said she would pay $25 for the portrait. Again, he said no. She persisted and offered to pay $50. While my friend thought a bit more about it, he still refused. However, when she said she would pay $100 (more money than he could imagine), he replied, "Under one condition, that I can leave my socks on so I've a place to keep my paint brushes." I thought Jordy was going to "split a gut," as he laughed until he nearly cried.

Once Jordy told me, he liked my smile, and that it made him feel good. He was an affectionate person. I'll always remember the first time he said he loved me. As I grasped his hand and gave him a hug, he uttered those marvelous words.

When I told Jordy, he was included in my book, he looked surprised, smiled and said, and "I can't believe an old 'codger' like me is going to be in a book." He then asked why I would write a book. I told him I needed the money. However, I didn't convince him that was my motive. Before I left for winter vacation, I instinctively knew I'd never see Jordy again and gave him a special hug. As I fought back tears, I repeated how much I loved him and how he had blessed my life.

"Greg's Different Perspective to Illness"

(There is a tendency to look for the good in people when they're ill and to disregard their flaws. Hospice staff and volunteers are good at this and so are family and friends as they put life in perspective. The sketch about Greg presents a different view of illness as he establishes cheerful relationships with people for the first time in his life.)

When I met Greg, I found out quickly what a unique person he was. He was upbeat and had a subtle sense of humor. He caught me by surprise when he said, "Cancer has been a gift to me and the illness has fulfilled my life." When I asked him why, he reported the treatment and care he received while ill restored his faith in people. He was amazed at the attention he received from perfect strangers and valued the relationships that developed.

Greg was very open as he talked about his background. He had an unhappy childhood and came from a dysfunctional family. He had one sister who he hadn't spoken to in years. As a young adult, Greg relied on substance abuse to escape. He was a loner and had few friends.

As I spoke with Greg, it was apparent he was a person of intellect and a deep thinker. He was a prolific reader and could converse on most any subject. When I learned he was a housekeeper at a facility, I was surprised. This remarkable man had so much to offer but had little opportunity to interact with others.

On Greg's arm was a tattoo that said "good" and "evil." I don't know what the significance was, but sensed it might have been difficult for him to distinguish between the two. He was not a person of faith, had a fear of pain and wanted help to prepare for death. Sister Sue spent time with him to deal with spiritual issues. One thing was certain; his time at the Home brought him contentment and the realization that people cared.

"Sid's Premature Plans"

(Hospice patients have lots of time to reflect on death and as it approaches, some have ambivalent feelings. One part of them wants to die while the other doesn't. For people of faith, while there is the anticipation of the life to come, sometimes doubts appear. Such was not the case with Sid. He was more than ready. His spirituality led to a number of humorous incidents as he made plans to expedite his death.)

Sid talked with pride about a wonderful family that included nine children—all highly successful. He appreciated his many quality years of life that spanned over nine decades. In his home, he displayed an old Irish proverb, "Do not resent growing old for many are denied the privilege."

Sid was gregarious by nature and had a multitude of friends. I enjoyed my visits as he generously shared his quick wit and sense of humor. He was a great conversationalist and a wonderful storyteller. A segment in his obituary said it best. "He could take the most mundane event of everyday life and weave it into a fascinating or funny story, often with a good moral to it."

Sid loved to reminisce about the "good old days" when he partied a bit. With a grin, he told about an evening with his wife and some of their friends. After a "happy hour" at one of their homes, they went out for dinner.

Sid, known for his generosity, often bought a round of drinks at the restaurant. However, this particular evening he declined for he thought his friends had already imbibed enough. He wanted them alert so they could do their strut on the dance floor after dinner. Sid's friends, a bit on the frugal side, expressed disappointment in his refusal to buy them a beverage—so uncharacteristic of him. After several unsuccessful attempts to get Sid to change his mind, they (accompanied by everyone in the bar) broke out into song. "Here we sit like birds in the wilderness, birds in the wilderness, and birds in the wilderness; here we sit like birds in the wilderness, Sid won't buy a drink." In spite of the pressure, he held his ground and didn't give in to their request.

As Sid's illness progressed, he talked about death and was ready to go. He was a religious man and had long ago made peace with his maker. However, patience wasn't one of his virtues. He had always been in charge and didn't hesitate to make decisions. As Sid was more than ready for the heavenly journey, he contacted his priest. In no uncertain terms, he stated, "Father, I want to die in two days. If you can't help me, I'm going to get someone else." When this approach failed, he made what he thought was his final decision when he requested, Gail, a hospice nurse, call the local funeral home and send a hearse to transport his body. In an attempt to delay the process and with the hope that he might change his mind, Gail suggested he eat lunch first. Sid complied and ate large portions of everything available—the usual occurrence. When finished, he again requested Gail call the funeral home.

Sister Sue intervened. She told Sid that God had a plan, and when the time was right, would call him home. Sid quickly responded, "I've given him plenty of time. I can't believe he's not ready yet." Several weeks later, as I fed Sid breakfast, I observed a quote on his t-shirt that said, "My goal is to live forever—so far so good." I didn't comment and continued to feed him. As usual, he ate a good breakfast. Later, I learned one of his daughters, in the true spirit of living, gave him the shirt. He enjoyed the gesture, displayed it for all to see and passed it on to a friend. The same sequence happened three more times. Finally, Sid's daughter told him her supplier had quit making the shirts and to hold on to the one he had. He complied. Another daughter affectionately said, "My dad was a real character right down to the last minute." Sid's family accepted his health condition and thoroughly enjoyed his company to the end. So did I.

"Leona and Stella's Special Relationship"

(During hospice care, some patients confide in each other and quickly become close friends. At this stage of their lives, there are few inhibitions. They willingly share the most personal and intimate aspects of their past and perceptions about dying. Such was the case with Leona and Stella.)

Leona was more outgoing and talkative than Stella was, but their personalities and interests meshed, and a lasting friendship ensued. They were constant companions and shared their innermost feelings. Each had a wonderful sense of humor and positive outlook on life. For them, the cup was half full.

They generally enjoyed my visits and typically greeted me with a smile and a "Happy Birthday." As they learned about my flaws, they enjoyed teasing me. Once when I took Leona back to her room, I made a wrong turn when exiting the hall. She smiled because she thought I erred intentionally to create a humorous moment. When I assured her my faulty sense of direction had flared up, her smile transformed into laughter.

On another occasion, as I prepared Stella for lunch, I struggled to fit her with a clothing protector (the politically correct term for a bib). She laughed in amazement and indicated she would assist me the next time I tried this simple task.

Both ladies loved nature and the plentiful flower gardens that surrounded the residence. Every week after lunch, I took them outside to enjoy creation's beauty. With each confined to a wheelchair, I alternated who would go first. After I transported one to the initial stop, a gazebo that overlooked a pond, I returned to get the other. Leona would often bring her bird book to help identify the many species that flew about, and Stella would watch the ducks as they glided on the water.

After the first shuttle, I devised a method to transport both ladies around the grounds at the same time. First, I'd take one a distance of 15-20 yards, and then go back and get the other. After we all enjoyed the landscape and exchanged some light conversation, I repeated the process. It took about ten of these sequences for our threesome to get around the grounds. Leona and Stella enjoyed the different views as we circled the property a couple of times. They would smile and say it was a good way for me to get some exercise!

One fall day on our stop at the Memorial Garden, Stella and Leona openly discussed dying and their mutual belief in life after death. They thought it would be nice to die about the same time. Although it was mid-October, they expressed a wish to make it through Christmas. While neither lived to celebrate the holy day, they died within a day of each other. That is with some divine intervention.

"Sing Again Rudy"

(The sketch about Rudy reinforces the power music can have to create happiness and contentment. He lived to sing but lost his voice due to illness. However, with practice, it returned, in part, and life was again worth living.)

Rudy, who suffered from progressive heart disease, resided in a nursing home where he received hospice services. He was a lonely man who seldom had visitors. Reportedly, his wife was in another nursing home, and his two children lived out of the area.

During my initial visit, he was in a lethargic state. His voice was weak, and it was a real effort for him to talk. This predicament, in combination with background noise, made it difficult to carry on a conversation. I later learned that he wasn't always confined to bed, and that this was his naptime. When we scheduled his visits at times when rested and alert, our conversations became productive.

I quickly learned that music was the love of Rudy's life. He had performed in choral groups, beginning in junior high school, and continued to sing into adulthood. He had a particular interest in opera, and his tenor voice graced a number of local productions. He lived for those magical moments on stage when the singing reflected excellence and captivated the audience. Rudy completely absorbed himself in the music, and other than hunting and fishing, had no other interests. When he became ill and was no longer able to sing, he became depressed and avoided social contact.

When I told Rudy I was a barbershop singer, he looked with interest and reported a liking for the a cappella style of music accompanied by close harmony. I capitalized on this interest and the following week brought a CD of my barbershop quartet. As he listened to the music, his eyes widened, and with a smile, began to mouth some of the words. He started to "come out of his shell" and reminisced about his musical experiences. Not only did he talk about professional performances, but also informal singing with close friends over a beverage or two.

As weeks followed, I played CDs of elite singing groups that included award winning barbershop quartets and choruses and southern gospel groups. Rudy enjoyed the music and became an active listener. As he moved his hands to the rhythm of the songs, he would hum. Later, much to Rudy's surprise, his singing voice returned for brief periods. However, the voice was weak and lacked quality—not up to his standards. Nonetheless, the accomplishment improved his spirits and provided motivation to sing again.

We discarded the CDs and transitioned to live singing. I quickly learned that Rudy enjoyed the old songs and retrieved my book of "golden oldies (quickly wearing out from excessive usage). Initially, Rudy's confidence level was low, and his attempts to sing lacked assertiveness. During this period, he exhibited frustration and made such comments as, "It's still (meaning his voice) not there yet;" "I don't have enough breath support;" "My voice comes and goes;" and "It's so frustrating not being able to sing well." However, Rudy displayed determination and kept trying.

With each week that followed, Rudy's voice became stronger as did his confidence level. Many of his comments changed from the cup being half empty to half full. In those brief moments when the melodious voice returned, he would smile and state, "That wasn't too bad;" "I surprised myself;" "I really liked that harmony;" "This is fun;" and "That's neat; I can holler again."

Some of the old songs resulted in great harmony as Rudy sang tenor and I filled in with the lead. Such classics as "Let the Rest of the World Go By," "I Want a Girl," "By the Light of the Silvery Moon," "Shine on Harvest Moon," "My Wild Irish Rose," and "On Moonlight Bay," brought Rudy personal satisfaction. As Rudy reacquired his singing voice (compromised as it was), a renewed spirit blessed his latter days. Our mutual interest in music bonded us together, and a wonderful friendship developed.

CHAPTER 8

Stories about My Friends with Terminal Illness

"Judy, Santa and More"

I first met my dear friend Judy when I had her as a student over 25 years ago. She possessed all those favorable attributes that a teacher loves: smart, great work ethic, conscientious, dedicated, humble and exemplary people skills. Judy had a passion for life and selfless demeanor seldom seen. Her concerns were always for others—family, friends and patients she served as a health care professional. She was special.

Judy developed cancer in her mid-forties. Initial treatment was successful, and the disease was in remission for a few years. However, an untreatable form returned. In spite of the terminal illness, Judy possessed an unimaginable will-to-live, and her smile and upbeat attitude persisted to the end.

For Judy's last Christmas, her colleagues had a surprise party in her honor. Even Santa (her old teacher incognito no less) made an appearance and with a vigorous "Ho-Ho-Ho," greeted Judy. Without hesitation and with a look of amusement, she jumped on the jolly old guy's lap and suggested he had put on a few pounds. Judy had not lost the good-natured teasing that endeared her to friends. As she conversed with Santa, she made small talk and submitted a wish list—all requests for others. During the special day, Judy was in rare form and good will prevailed.

During illness, Judy continued graduate studies and earned a doctorate in audiology. In the presence of family, friends and colleagues, she received the honor while hospitalized. When the dean of the graduate school conferred the degree, Dr. Judy smiled and asked, "Does that mean I get a raise?" She never lost her sense of humor.

Judy was deeply religious and had a spiritual presence. When she became sick, she collected angels and received a number as gifts from friends. These symbols reminded Judy of her faith and hope for life to come. Shortly before her death, she looked lovingly at her mom and dad and with a smile said, "There's an angel behind each of you." This revelation convinced Judy her parents would be cared for and gave her peace of mind.

Judy had a terrific support system: a devoted husband, two loving children, caring parents and dedicated friends. While she appreciated everyone's support, she still worried about her family and how they would adjust to her passing.

Judy had a knack for bringing out the best in people. When in her presence, one smiled and felt good. While others recognized her engaging qualities, Judy did not and underestimated the impact she had on others. At her funeral, the calling line stretched to the parking lot, and there was standing room only at the service. I was one of many that proudly delivered eulogies. Smiles and tears abounded for the special person who truly made a difference.

Shortly after Judy's passing, a large plaster of Paris piggy bank, with quite a history, appeared. Judy, along with two childhood friends, made the coin collector when at Girl Scout camp. As her friend cleaned the basement of her home, she came across the dated treasure and passed it on. The timing could not have been better for Judy's daughter was involved in a pig-wrestling contest that very day. At the end of the muddy event, she received a special gift from her mother—a touching moment.

While it's been four years since Judy's passing, her memory is alive and well. Friends continue to reflect on the impact she had on their lives. Every year one special friend sends a note to Judy's parents in honor of her birthday. Her legacy is intact.

"Terry the Jokester and the Fishing Experience"

Terry was a good friend for over 40 years. We shared many of the same interests, sang in a barbershop quartet together and enjoyed each other's company. He was fun loving, had a terrific sense of humor and a robust laugh that caught everyone's attention. When he became ill with an invasive form of cancer, he was determined to beat the disease and fought it to the end. He squeezed as much life as he could in the time he had left.

When Terry sang in our barbershop quartet in the 1970s, he often told a joke or two. He so enjoyed his stories, more so than the audience did, when the only laughter heard was his. One time he got off to a wrong start and talked about an "alligator purse" rather than, what should have been, "alligator shoes." While I can't recall all the specifics, the punch line was, "He (meaning the alligator) wasn't wearing any shoes."—not a good fit with purse. The rest of the quartet knew Terry was in trouble from the start and laughed throughout the story. Admittedly, we were a bit sadistic, looked forward to the disastrous conclusion, and weren't disappointed. When Terry realized his fate, his robust laughter echoed throughout the auditorium as the audience gazed in confusion. However, Terry never became discouraged when his stories "laid an egg." He was a good sport and enjoyed the sequels. That's all that mattered. Even when ill, he remained undaunted and continued to tell tales, much to his enjoyment.

Terry was an avid outdoorsman and loved to fish and hunt on his 30 acres of wooded land that included several hundred feet of lake frontage. This is where we shared many fishing experiences. Shortly before his death, he took me fishing one final time. Although in pain, he insisted on driving, as he never trusted my navigation skills. Off we went on the 35-mile trip to his "paradise on earth." As we traveled, the conversation was light and upbeat. Talk about sports, current events, family and even a few of his classic stories made it a short trip. When we entered the lane that lead to the lakefront, I wondered what went through his mind. He struggled to get out of the car, and with considerable effort and discomfort, walked the rocky path to the fishing dock.

Terry never complained about his physical condition and only talked about the fish he was about to catch. Importantly, he was still in charge and not dependent on others. In spite of having fished together many times, he remained generous in his advice for this inferior angler. He criticized my cast, and suggested I had too much movement from the arm and not enough from the wrist. As I recognized his guru status, I complied.

In that the fish were not biting from the location he suggested, I moved my position to the far side of the dock. With self-assuredness, he told me there were no fish in that area, and I would likely snag the line in the rocks and brush. On my first cast, I hooked a white bass and proudly reeled it in. As Terry watched the catch, he shook his head in disbelief.

When I caught another fish with the second cast, he ignored the feat and kept fishing. Finally, when I made it 3/3, Terry pushed me aside and took my spot. However, even with the change of location, results were the same. To make matters worse, when he did catch a fish, it was smaller than mine.

Terry was at his wits end. Now I was in charge. With a smirk, I pointed out a few flaws in his technique that he needed to correct. That really set him off. After a few expletives, he reeled in his line, and we headed for home with 65 white bass. In that Terry did not have any faith in my filleting skills, he insisted that he clean the catch. I don't know who ever ate the fish. Perhaps, they are still in his family's freezer.

In spite of Terry's declining health, I treated him the same way as I always had. Our relationship thrived on good-natured teasing, and this incident was a perfect opportunity to continue that trend. The experience was therapeutic for Terry for he was totally consumed with something he liked. It really didn't matter who made the catch—maybe a little. We laughed all the way home about my lucky day. To no one's surprise, he never gave me any credit! Friends are friends in health and illness.

"Will the Financial Guru"

I met Will through his wife, a professional colleague and friend. I made my visits to his home where he received the best of care from a devoted wife. Although Will and I had different personalities and interests, we hit it off well and became good friends. He was ill with an aggressive form of cancer. While doctors gave him no more than three months, he defied the odds, much to the amazement of the medical community, and lived another five plus years. He had a remarkable attitude, positive outlook on life and made every day count. Even as his health deteriorated, he never talked about his physical condition. While not an outgoing person, he had a subtle sense of humor that he shared as our friendship developed. I so enjoyed my time with him.

Will was a private person not much for words. That is unless you talked about the stock market. Then he would carry on a conversation for hours at a time. He had an amazing amount of information that he shared willingly. He had studied trends in the stock market for many years and was a successful investor. He idolized Warren Buffett for whom he credited his financial security.

Will and I would frequently lunch at a local restaurant to discuss investment strategies. The owner became one of Will's biggest fans. He not only appreciated the boost in business, but the investment tips as well—cheap at twice the price. As Will gave advice, patrons would gather. They listened intently, took notes and asked questions. Will was the teacher, and we were the students. After several visits to the establishment, I became selfish and did not want to share Will's gems with others—just kidding of course. I was happy to see him in his element as he had the time of his life. It was good therapy.

As an investor with little experience, I showed my ignorance. I thought the S & P was a grocery chain and had difficulty grasping the lingo of the stock market. However, Will accepted the challenge and displayed more patience than I deserved. He went out of his way to explain concepts in different ways—with graphs and even the *Wall Street Journal*. When Will did get something across to this slow learner, you could observe a sense of pride that he had accomplished something special. I got the idea he felt if he could teach me, he could teach anyone. Importantly, when in his element, Will was happy and nothing else mattered. Even in his latter days when bedridden, he would give me a reading assignment or stock tip and then quiz me the next time we met. I never saw him so happy when I explained what constituted a balanced portfolio.

I miss Will's advice, particularly in the gloom and doom times of a recession; but most of all, I miss Will.

Not only was he a financial guru, he was a good person. He loved the simple pleasures of life. He was a nature lover and was in heaven when in the outdoors of northern Wisconsin in virgin forests and crystal lakes where he kept company with eagles and loons. He was a special guy.

"Chad's Indefatigable Faith and Spirit"

(People of faith often deal with terminal illness with a positive outlook and anticipation of a new life to come. Even as death nears, humor persists and life, while compromised, goes on without regrets. Chad's story highlights these compelling qualities.)

Chad, a dear friend from church, possessed an upbeat attitude, terrific sense of humor and a love for life that brought out the best in everyone. He was an exemplary Christian who always gave to others. When diagnosed with cancer, to no one's surprise, Chad kept a positive frame of mind. He relied on faith and prayer, as well as support from family and friends, to sustain him. After successful treatment and surgery, the cancer was in remission.

Even before Chad contracted cancer, he was an active volunteer and served on the county board of the American Cancer Society (ACS). He attended meetings with state and federal lawmakers and served as an advocate for cancer patients and their families. After illness, he worked with the ACS's Relay for Life program at local and national levels and raised thousands of dollars for the cause. He, along with his wife and soul mate Kelly, became actively involved in Bosom Buddies, a local cancer support group. About four years after the initial diagnosis, Chad again experienced pain and discomfort. He subsequently went to the Mayo Clinic where they discovered a rare form of invasive cancer and performed surgery. With a guarded prognosis and high likelihood of recurrence, he returned home determined to make the best of the situation.

Chad had been an avid biker before illness and desired to continue the hobby. In view of his physical limitations, he purchased a semi-recumbent bike and made the most of the opportunities to use it. As he toured the neighborhood, grateful he could move the pedals, he smiled and waved to all. While this activity was short-lived because of failing health, Chad continued to live and cherished his last vestiges of independence.

Chad diligently appeared for weekly breakfast with the men of the church (which included me) and did his part to solve the world's problems—with a bit of brevity I might add. During these times, he continued to display a signature smile, sense of humor and never complained about his physical condition. Chad loved to tease me, as do most of my friends. However, he exceeded the limits of most and received undue pleasure when he delivered a zinger. He really liked to challenge my biased analyses of Milwaukee Brewers' baseball players. I was particularly critical of their second baseman, one of Chad's favorite players. When our budding super star had an occasional good game, I really got the treatment at breakfast. As the ringleader, Chad would orchestrate the teasing, and the rest of the guys would follow. The ribbing was brutal, and my credibility as a baseball analyst took a hit.

When Chad's condition declined, he returned to the Mayo Clinic and had more surgery. The doctors gave him a few months to live and an option to buy time with treatment. He chose against treatment, but not against living. With a terrific wife and supportive family who were always there for him, he got the most out of life, as compromised as it was. He loved visits from friends, was at peace, and openly talked about his faith and the life to come. Once as he talked about death, he smiled and said, "When I get up there, I'm going to have a talk with him and ask what the problem is."

When my barbershop group sang for Chad, he thanked everyone for the visit and with a devilish smile stated, "You have my sympathies for including Jack in the group." When I told him, we had another stop to sing for one of my friends, he responded, "I didn't know you had any friends." As we left, Chad opened the door and shouted "Happy Birthday!" It was almost like a rebirth and a heavenly moment—how appropriate I thought.

As Chad's condition worsened, I would often call to have a chat. Once after a snowstorm, I asked him how he was adapting. He laughed and stated he wasn't concerned about the Wisconsin weather for he was in Florida to enjoy the sun. He persisted and just about had me convinced. The teasing/prankster part of Chad never left, and I loved him for it.

When diagnosed with cancer the second time, Chad chronicled his remarkable journey of his final days and shared his thoughts and feelings by email with friends— many in his cancer support group. He spoke candidly about how he dealt with terminal illness and the hope of things to come. I've included excerpts from his updates as related to "condition," "faith," and "humor." As his condition worsened, faith became stronger and sense of humor remained intact.

01/05/08

Condition—"Kelly and I are back from Mayo Clinic. They found a malignant peripheral nerve sheath tumor (MPNST) located between my hip and knee. Since this is a very aggressive form of cancer, they wanted to start treatment as soon as possible."

Faith—"Kelly and I want to thank you for all the cards and prayers. They help so very much."

Humor—"I will have a PET scan. I don't know what pet they will use, but I hope it doesn't bite."

01/20/08

<u>Condition</u>—"I had surgery Jan. 11th and the team of doctors removed the tumor, a section of the sciatica nerve and two hamstrings in the upper leg. I have very little pain but do have a phantom pain in my foot. It is strange because the nerve connection to the foot has been severed. So the pain is really in my mind."

<u>Faith</u>—"I really believe in the power of prayers. God does hear and respond to them. I have seen proof of his might, power and guidance. Keep us in your thoughts and prayers, and we will make it through the next set of treatments."

01/30/08

<u>Condition</u>—"I just returned from seeing the doctor at a local clinic. He pulled one drain and took out about half of the stitches. I go back Friday when he will remove the rest of the stitches and the last drain. That's going to feel great. I'm doing very well otherwise. I still don't have pain around the surgery wound. It is uncomfortable to sit on, but I can do it for short periods of time. My friend Jerry made a ramp so now it's much easier to get out of the house. I can get up and down without any trouble. Kelly doesn't want me going any place other than the doctor's office. She doesn't think I'm real stable in the walker and one leg. We both are concerned I might fall."

Faith—"Please keep me in your prayers. I have a long way to go but am making progress. God heard your prayers because he has me on the mend."

Humor—"Kelly has taken such good care of me so I listen to her and try to follow orders. Notice I said, 'Try'."

03/15/08

Condition—"I'm having an easy time with the treatments. I have some hair loss in the area they've been treating and a little redness in each end of the surgery wounds. I'm wearing a compression sock that Kelly has to put on for me. I can reach my foot, but there is no way I can get the sock on. I still get a lot of swelling. They say radiation may be the partial cause of it. The swelling in back is the worst part for it hinders the movement of my leg when walking. A good piece of news is I can ride the stationary bike as long as I find a way to hold my foot on the pedals. I can even push with that leg but so far can't pull very much."

Faith—"I will never be able to thank Kelly enough for all that she has done. I keep telling her how much I love her, and that the best thing that God did was put her in my life. God has been good to us for putting so many caring friends in our lives. It's been a tough challenge for us but, with your help and God's, we have made it through. I don't know what the future has in store for us, but I know it will be a heck of a ride."

Humor— "'Where is your cane?' I hear that a lot from Kelly. When I forget to grab the cane, she tells me that she is going to strike. If I don't listen, I am down!"

08/07/08

Condition—"I had a great time with my grandsons at this year's Experimental Aircraft Association Fly-In. They really made my week. Then things turned bad when Kelly and I went to Mayo Clinic for my 3-month checkup. They found a tumor in the back of the leg that they did surgery on in January. They're not sure whether it's malignant so they'll do a biopsy. They also found a tumor in my lungs that they are really concerned about." (Note: Biopsies on the lungs and leg showed cancer and surgeries were performed on each. Neither radiation nor chemotherapy were recommended following surgery.)

Faith—"The news hit Kelly and me pretty hard but we are dealing with it and hoping and praying that things will turn out for the best. I know God will be with us through this challenge as well."

09/29/08

Condition—"I'm doing well and do not plan on returning to the Mayo Clinic unless something really goes wrong. Check-ups every 3-months will be done locally. I search on the Internet for more information but there is not much out there for this type of cancer. I'm not one to try off-the-wall cures or prevention supplements but a friend of Kelly's gave us Essiac tea to try which has had a long history in Canada. Her husband had used it in a bout with pancreatic cancer. I ran it by my family doctor and he said to give it a try. He did not see any harm in it because I'm not under any other treatment for cancer at this time. It's supposed to strengthen the immune system as well as destroy cancer cells in the body. We'll see what happens."

Faith—"I feel I have found peace with it all. It's not that I've quit fighting, but I have to accept what the future has for me. I know that Jesus will be by my side supporting me and giving me strength that I need. It's hard to put into words how I feel when I let my mind dwell on this. I can tell you that the prayers and good wishes are felt by me every day. That's part of the support and strength that God provides."

Humor—"I started driving again and last week was my first behind the wheel; so now Kelly can't keep me home!"

11/20/08

Condition—"All my tests are in and we now know all the sordid details. The tumors are back and they are very aggressive. Surgery has been ruled out as an option, and I am not in favor of doing chemo to just buy a few months at most and destroy the quality of life I have left. I am comfortable with what we have heard. They told me my life expectancy is less than a year depending on how fast the tumors grow. They should be able to keep me comfortable to the end. Kelly and I have accepted this and will deal with it."

Faith—"Kelly and I know that the Lord will walk with me the last stage of my life, and I will be with him forever. I know God will give us the strength we need. I thank all of you for the prayers. If you see me somewhere, please feel free to come up and give me a hug. I can never get enough of them."

Humor—"I can still laugh, joke and smile so things are fine."

12/06/08

Condition—"I visited the doctors yesterday to see if there is any relief I could get for the cough that I have when talking. X-ray pictures showed the left lung is full of fluid. They plan to drain it next week. The tumors are growing pretty fast. They've almost doubled in size in a month."

Faith—"It is better to trust the Lord than put confidence in man." (Psalm 118:8). How true that statement is. I am very thankful I have family and friends to support Kelly and me. I feel the love, caring and prayers every day. Most importantly, I have Christ on my side to give me strength. Jesus reserved a room for me in God's house and all I have to do is pick up the "key." I have the key in my heart, which is comfort beyond explanation."

Humor—"Kelly and I can still laugh and joke around and hug each other when things are tough. She has been so good to me but as she said the other night, "You're getting on thin ice.""

12/13/08

Condition—"I had my lung drained which has helped my breathing. Kelly and I are learning many things about the final stages of life. We have registered for palliative care instead of hospice at this time. Palliative care will allow me to see a doctor to have the lung drained when needed. We can change to hospice any time. I will get visits from the VNA staff on a scheduled basis and as needed between visits. There is a lot of comfort in knowing there is that support out there. We have a tank of oxygen as a back up in the house if needed to help with my breathing."

<u>Faith</u>—"I had a wonderful visit from a very old friend from high school days. We had a wonderful time talking about our lives. We had some great times together when young and full of life. It is interesting how our lives have had the same twists and turns, and how we both have ended up with God as the center of our lives now. He brought me a book titled *Heaven* by Randy Alcorn. He talks about what heaven will be like based on information in the Bible. I have not skipped ahead but would like to get a better understanding of what he has to say. I have tried to stay positive through this final journey. It is easy to let the mind move away from what I need to focus on right now. I find reading really helps. The Holy Spirit works in many ways but is always there to help. All I have to do is ask. What a blessing it is to know Christ and to know, that through him, I have a place in heaven. It is something to really look forward to. As this earthly life comes to an end, I feel so lucky to have my faith in God's forgiveness and that with that forgiveness, I will have a never-ending life in heaven. Thanks for all your prayers and support. They keep me warm just thinking about them."

12/20/08

<u>Condition</u>—"I now have a drain in my chest. Kelly will learn to drain me next Monday. I'm having some discomfort for which I'm taking medications."

Faith—"I'm about half through the book, *Heaven*. I'm having a nice time painting my own picture of what it will be like. I'm sure I cannot paint a picture that will be even close. But that's okay. It helps me to be wrapped in the love for Jesus Christ."

Humor—"This morning I've been having hot flashes. Oh! What fun it is."

12/26/08

Condition—"I've been having some pain but the medications are controlling it. It has been a Catch-22 with pain medications causing an upset stomach."

Faith—"I could not make it to God's house for worship but said my prayers at home. What a wonderful gift God gave us that first Christmas night. With that gift, I know I will rejoice with Jesus in heaven."

Humor—"I even had a visit from Santa. He sure is a tall man!"

Sometimes one has an opportunity to say goodbye while the patient is still alert and conversant. The conditions need to be right and the patient needs to accept that death is near. Such was the case with Chad. Shortly before I left for vacation in December, I said my goodbyes and wrote this note to him.

"Thanks for your friendship. You are a special person who can anticipate a front row seat in heaven. Even in illness, you have lived an exemplary life with a strong faith and positive attitude. I will always remember your terrific sense of humor, warm smile and will miss the teasing by the master. I will look forward to seeing you in a better place. Take care good friend and have a heavenly birthday and a new beginning."

On January 19, 2009, they admitted Chad to a local nursing home to spend his final days. Morphine controlled pain, and oxygen helped him to breathe. While he no longer had the strength to talk for sustained periods, he remained alert and loved to have visitors. He was in good spirits and still had a sense of humor. His trust in God became even stronger (if that's possible) and he anticipated the trip to heaven. God granted his wish on February 6th with Kelly and their children at his side.

"Judge Rick's Passion for Humor and Song"

Rick was one of the first people I met in 1966 when we moved from Ohio to Wisconsin. Right from the start, he knew of the exploits of "Killer" on the gridiron and the nickname stuck. We had many mutual interests, most notably barbershop quartet singing and our families became close friends. He had a quick wit and terrific sense of humor. He loved a good joke and was a great storyteller. Nothing made Rick happier than making others smile.

Rick was an attorney and served as a circuit court judge for over 20 years. He had a brilliant mind, an excellent reputation, and his peers recognized him as being exceedingly fair. He and his wife Mary made the most of their retirement years and thoroughly enjoyed their family. He had many friends and truly made a difference.

For over 50 years, Rick sang in barbershop quartets. He loved a cappella singing in harmony and was good at it. He used his creative talents to write parodies and slap stick comedies for his quartets. He was funny, his quartets were funny and they thrived on laughter. On occasion, when court was in recess, Judge Rick would break out in song. It broke the tension. At Rick's retirement party, not only was Wisconsin's Chief Supreme Court Justice present, so was Rick's barbershop quartet. Both received equal billing.

Early in our friendship, Rick became aware of my many flaws that included my inability to accomplish any task that required any semblance of mechanical or manual aptitude. He exploited my deficiencies and teased me unmercifully. A classic story, which he shared to many over the past 35 years, involved my one-time experience as a roofer. Lee, another barbershop friend invited me (for some unknown reason) to assist him and Rick in installing a new roof on his lakefront cottage. Reluctantly, I accepted, but knew I was doomed for failure.

(Upon my arrival, Lee directed me to the work location, and demonstrated how to nail and line up shingles. Next, he gave me a carpenter's apron, a hammer and some nails. We positioned ourselves on the roof, Rick on one end, Lee on the other and me in the middle. After three rows were finished, Lee initiated a quality control check. He and Rick lined up the shingles with a purple chalked line, and each grabbed an end. When Lee snapped the string, the color appeared as expected. However, the tracing, while straight on both ends, was off course in the middle. Lee, in a huff, ripped off the shingles I had so carefully laid. After some deliberation with Rick, Lee reluctantly gave me a second chance and repeated the instructions interspersed with a few expletives. We all regained our spots on the roof and resumed the work. After three more rows were completed, Lee repeated the dreaded test with the same results. While Rick laughed hysterically, Lee was livid. It was two and out. I was relieved of my duties and forced to return the hammer and apron.

At the close of the day, Lee requested I perform one job he thought even I could accomplish. That was to cut a shingle in half so it was flush with the end of the roof. To accomplish the task, he gave me a ruler, pencil and heavy-duty scissors. I measured carefully as I didn't want to fail again. With pride, I presented Lee with a half a shingle. Lee, out of character, doubled up with laughter and Rick joined in. Both came close to falling off the roof. I had cut the shingle the wrong way. I slowly exited the roof demoralized.)

At my retirement party roast, Rick shared the infamous incident with a few embellishments. I feigned a look of shock and disgust as he described the gory details. Shortly before his death, he brought the story up "out of the blue" and with a grin suggested I consider roofing as a part time job to pass idle time.

For a number of years, Rick battled health problems. He survived an initial bout with cancer. However, he couldn't beat, hard as he tried, a more invasive form a few years later. Even with the realization that he was dying, Rick remained himself. About a month before he died, I drove him to the hospital for a radiation treatment. As I tried to back out of his driveway (a winding labyrinth that I always had trouble negotiating), he smiled and said, "You never did learn how to do it." He was right. I never did.

During the 80-mile journey, Rick was his usual jovial self and told a story or two as only he could do. We even engaged in some two-part harmony as we sang some barbershop favorites. While Rick's voice was weak, it was right on pitch—a requirement of his. Much like Terry ("Terry the Jokester and the Fishing Experience"), Rick didn't complain about the pain or discuss his illness. It was a typical Rick and "Killer" experience. While his illness didn't affect the fun, several impromptu naps during the trip made me increasingly aware of his fragile condition.

Even in the advanced stages of illness, Rick would send me and a few other cronies daily emails of a jocular nature. I received my last on-line correspondence from Rick about three weeks before his passing. It was entitled "A Cow, an Ant and an Old Fuddy-Duddy." The Cow: "I give 50 liters of milk every day. That's why I am the greatest!" The Ant: "I work day and night, summer and winter. I can carry 52 times my own weight. That's why I am greatest!" There was no quote from the "Old Fuddy-Duddy." As I scrolled down the computer monitor, I came across the statement, "It's your turn to say something."

I visited Rick the day he died. He was at home where he wanted to be with his devoted wife and children. Hospice had provided a bed in the sunroom. While still conscious, he was unable to speak. However, his mind was as sharp as ever. He held out his hand, and we touched. I flashed my "Killer" football stance, and he managed a smile. He still had his sense of humor.

Rick's funeral was a celebration of life and music was a significant part of the memorial service. A multitude of barbershoppers came to pay their respects and sang in a mass chorus in Rick's memory. Rick's granddaughter blessed the service with her beautiful singing voice. Family, friends and colleagues presented reflections of his life. They highlighted his compassion and caring for others and his special sense of humor.

CHAPTER 9

Stories about Patients from Friends and Hospice Volunteers

"Bert and Bart's Humor"

(My friend Pastor Bob told me of this incident that involved Bert and Bart, both with terminal illnesses. The episode involves the spontaneous exchange of humor considered inappropriate in most social situations. However, it suggests, when both giver and receiver have terminal illness, there is a different standard to tease and joke. There are few restrictions and political correctness is not an issue.)

Both Bert and Bart, long time friends, had terminal illnesses. Bert possessed an invasive respiratory disorder and an oxygen tank was his constant companion. Bart had a progressive cancer and was in perpetual pain. In spite of poor health, they were good-natured and still had fun. They had their "bucket lists" and were determined to squeeze as much into life in the time they had left.

Bert and Bart were members of a card club that met monthly to play sheepshead, a trick-taking game with a German origin and commonly played in Wisconsin. Players generally take the game seriously and competition is keen. For these friends with illness, the night out took on added significance. It was good therapy. As in many card groups, playful ribbing occurs, and this sheepshead group was no exception. While Bart was a master player, Bert was a novice prone to mistakes. However, he knew his limitations and tolerated the abuse when teased.

One evening, after Bert made yet another indefensible error (at least in Bart's mind), Bart directed a few terse comments to his pal, then grabbed his oxygen line and said, "You do that again and I'm going to pinch this thing off." Ordinarily, such a response would be tasteless and inappropriate. However, in this case, the giver, also with terminal illness, consumed by the moment, took action. Fortunately, Bert saw the humor and reacted with laughter. These dying men had a special bond that entitled them to openness and a "no-holds-barred" approach.

Had a healthy person in the group been involved in the episode, it would have likely taken on a different meaning.

"Ted's Last Hunt"

Pastor Bob described another incident with his good friend Ted who had a terminal illness. Through the years, they spent lots of time together as they hunted, fished, played cards, told stories, talked religion and lived life to the fullest. As Ted's condition worsened, Pastor planned one last outdoor activity for his dying friend. Since Ted was an avid goose hunter, it seemed like a good idea to plan such an expedition. He chose a special spot in an area marsh where the prized creatures were plentiful. In preparation for the hunt, Pastor received clearance from the Department of Natural Resources to drive Ted to a special spot ordinarily accessed by foot. He got the key to open the gate and transported his dear friend by car to the "firing line."

Ted, no longer able to stand for sustained periods, positioned himself on a five-gallon bucket. With considerable effort, he loaded the gun and eagerly waited. Meanwhile, Pastor Bob drove his jeep back to the parking lot and then returned to join Ted. Suddenly, he saw a wave of geese. When Pastor Bob knelt down on the road, he observed the geese as they flew towards Ted, positioned to take a shot. As the flock flew over, Ted raised his shotgun and reflexively shot a couple of times. Because of his weakened condition, he fell from the stool as the shots flew aimlessly. When Pastor Bob came to Ted's side, he found him lying on the ground with no fowl for his efforts, but hardly important in this case. As they laughed and hugged, things could not have been better.

What an appropriate way for special friends to say goodbye. Pastor Bob shared the story at Ted's funeral. He added that Ted was not afraid of death, but fearful that he would lose friends. Pastor assured Ted that God's plan most likely included a reunion with his pals. That gave Ted peace of mind, and he was ready to meet his maker.

"Darla's Special Hug"

(There was a time when a hug was a well-accepted gesture to show that you care. While many continue to make generous use of this action (me included), others fail to do so for a myriad of reasons. I come from a family of huggers and the action has always been a natural, spontaneous thing for me to do. I can generally sense for whom the action is appropriate. The sketch below exemplifies the positive aspects of hugs, with a humorous element, between a hospice volunteer and the son of a patient.)

Volunteers often share hugs with hospice patients and their families. When Darla, a hospice volunteer, finished a visit with Carl, a patient, she gave him a hug. Before she left, Carl reported his son was on the way to visit him and requested she also give him a hug. As Darla was about to leave the building, she a saw a young man that fit the son's description and acted as instructed. However, as she conversed with the gentleman, she soon realized it was a case of mistaken identity. While the "huggee" seemed to take it well, Darla still suffered from the embarrassment that she had hugged the wrong person.

Later Darla learned the young man also had a father who was a patient. The next week she learned the man's father had just died. With some apprehension and un-easiness, Darla approached the deceased's room to pay her respects. When she arrived, the son greeted her with a smile, extended his arms and gave her a hug. He knew she cared.

"Chet's Amazing Grace"

(In this sketch, Katie, a volunteer at the Home, writes passionately about the special relationship she developed with a patient. The heartwarming story about Chet has a personal and spiritual side, not void of humor, and covers a full range of emotions. It highlights how extraordinary people, such as Katie, bless the lives of others.)

"As a volunteer, I was excited about getting my first as-signment. Sure enough, there came an opening to help in the kitchen at the Hospice Home. All I had to do was ask the patient his/her preference for breakfast, write it down, and then give the order to our cook. My first order quick-ly taught me to never take a job of a waitress for granted

—apple juice with no ice, whole wheat toast with butter and jam (not jelly), cream of wheat with brown sugar, ('Is there any dessert left over from last night?'), coffee with two creams, and don't forget the ice water was my first order. Back at the kitchen, I could only think of a hot fudge sundae, hold the whipped cream. Thankfully, they taught us to write down orders because it's a long, humiliating walk back to the rooms to get them repeated."

"My second order went much easier. I knocked on the door, introduced myself, stated my purpose and quietly entered the room. There in the chair sat a perfectly groomed man who looked fresh and smelled of aftershave. Everything in the room had a place, and the bed sheets were smooth and tight. I just had my first encounter with Chet. He looked up, gave me half a smile, then lowered his head and said, 'I'll have an egg sunny side up and a piece of toast. If there's a donut, I'll have that too. No hurry, I'm just sitting here.' I couldn't wait to fill his order and get it back to him. There was just something special about this man that touched my heart."

"I made it through the breakfast shift without many mistakes. Thankfully, these precious patients are forgiving and willing to give the volunteer another chance. I remained on the breakfast "chain gang" for several weeks always looking forward to seeing Chet. So when I got the call asking to sit with him once a week while he went outside to smoke, I jumped at the chance. Every patient has a story to tell and I wanted to hear his."

"Bundling up for a smoke outside in a Wisconsin winter can take some time: flannel shirt, fleece jacket, coat, gloves, cap, blanket, pack of cigarettes, lighter and a cup of coffee. He got in his motorized wheelchair that he would maneuver himself, thank you, and out we headed. I was nervous since he seemed a bit stern, so I prayed that the Lord would give me the words he needed to hear and the wisdom and strength to deliver them. I remember thinking, 'He's so warm and cozy; he'll just fall asleep for sure.' But he proved me wrong."

"I opened the conversation with a joke, He laughed but remained quiet, more methodical than anything. I asked about his work, and he gave me a brief synopsis. When telling me he was a Marine, I patted his hand and thanked him for his sacrifice to keep our country free and safe. He looked at me, squinting one eye from the smoke and said, 'I don't understand how your husband would let you come and sit with another man.' I told him this was different. I was there because I didn't want him to be alone and for whatever the reason, we had a connection."

"Chet then began opening his life's book. This dear man had lost his sweetheart of 40 years, quite suddenly, ten years ago, and since then rarely left his home. He had four wonderful sons who were the joy of his life. Chet had lived through the Great Depression wearing cardboard shoes. He remembered breaking a bottle of Evening in Paris perfume he had purchased for his mother and that a lady, feeling sorry for him, gave him a dollar to replace it.

He helped his grandfather and father build a cabin. Chet loved the Packers and Brewers. Having a love for fishing, he, his wife and boys would fish from sunup to sundown and lunch on sandwiches made from a single loaf of bread. It was quickly evident that this man had a gentle spirit and broken heart."

"The more he shared, the more I found we had in common. Although 17 years apart in age, his life experiences were similar to my father's and I had an easy time listening to his stories. He was extremely intelligent and an avid reader. My one-hour-a-week assignment quickly turned to 3-4 hours three times a week. I watched as his shield of protection gradually wore away."

"Hospice addresses both the physical and spiritual needs of the patient. I knew Chet's physical needs were being filled, but where was he spiritually? Was he cynical, bitter, afraid, I had to ask. During my fourth visit, after Chet settled in with his smoke and coffee, my heart had to ask, 'When a person dies and they say, she passed; where do you think they go?' He slowly took a drag from his cigarette, blew it out, looked at me and said, 'I don't know.' I then asked if he believed in God or even if there was a heaven. This man had read and studied practically every religion known to man. This was his quandary, too much information. He was over thinking the simplest of questions."

"'Forget what you've read. Tell me from your heart,' I said. I wasn't there to sell one religion over another. I simply wanted him to find peace, a peace that passes all understanding. From then on, our discussions became more precious. I was getting to know the real Chet. God was opening doors and pouring out blessings I could never imagine."

"The residence was going through a mini-makeover, and some of the items, not in use, were set out for a drawing. Chet put his name on everything from a camera tripod to stools to ceramic angels. Surely, the odds were good that he'd win something. Well, he did. Tucked in the corner was a small brass church with a music box that played the song "Amazing Grace." During my next visit, he was holding that little church and examining it carefully. He said, 'It took a lot of work to make this. I thought of you when I saw it, and I want you to have it.' "

"Tears are welling in my eyes as I write this. I've been given many beautiful gifts in my life but this church from my precious friend is the most treasured one. From that time on, every time we met I would place my church on a chair next to us. He would smile that smile that would make his eyes twinkle. I'd kiss him on the forehead and say, 'I love you dear friend.' He would never respond."

"As the illness continued to take its toll and the medications increased, Chet began sleeping during our visits. I would continue talking as though he could still hear me. (My husband also sleeps when I'm talking, so it didn't bother me.) One time when I brought a Frank Sinatra CD for him to listen to, he opened his eyes and said, 'I thought we were going to have church.' He <u>had</u> been listening!"

"Once, Chet fell in his room. After the nurses attended to him and placed an alarm in his room, he phoned and asked if I wanted to come over and have coffee. He sounded scared and a bit shaken so I rushed to see him—breaking several traffic laws in the process. Although I had just seen him the day before, he looked so frail. I knew I would soon see my friend bedridden. My heart was breaking."

"A few weeks later, Chet fell again. This one put him in bed. I was visiting my 89-year-old mother in Louisville, Kentucky, when I heard of his falling. My husband and I returned home in record time to see him. It was a cold, rainy April evening when I entered Chet's room. He was on his side in bed surrounded by his sons. You and I could only hope to have sons like these. They were among the finest men I had ever met. Chet had told me so much about them I could name them without having seen them before. The room was so full of love it was overwhelming."

"Chet's breathing was shallow and his eyes closed. I held his hand, and let him know it was okay if he had to go. I felt a slight squeeze. I was going to be sad and miss him terribly but it would be all right. Soon he was going to see his precious sweetheart. He was going to be strong again and able to give her the biggest hug. The boat was ready to go fishing and was packed with sandwiches and a bucket of night crawlers."

"Fighting back tears, I told Chet how dear he was to me and that I brought my church. Quietly, I sang "Amazing Grace." As I got up to leave, I said, 'I'll either see you tomorrow or in heaven, whichever comes first. I love you.' I then kissed him on the forehead and said goodbye. A whisper came out of him, 'I love you too.' He died surrounded by his sons he loved so much."

"It was a great honor for me to sing "Amazing Grace" at Chet's "Homegoing" service. It took a while for the hole in my heart to close. Chet will always be a part of me. **He had become so alive during his time of dying.** I know he was a gift from God."

"A Special Goodbye from Alice"

(When the person with illness is both nonverbal and developmentally disabled, there are additional communication barriers, and to establish rapport and make connections can be problematic. In this account, Joyce, a devoted hospice volunteer and astute behavioral observer with remarkable intuitive skills, describes a special moment when communication occurred with a patient who had a severe developmental disability.)

Joyce, a hospice volunteer, described special moments with Alice who was developmentally disabled. Reportedly, Alice was healthy and active until the age of 20 when she developed seizure activity. Following treatment with electro-shock, she lost voluntary control of her body, could no longer walk or speak and required a feeding tube. For over 40 years, Alice resided in an institution. When she developed cancer in her 60s, she moved to a group home where she received personalized care and hospice services. During her five-month stay at this facility, her sister Jane visited her daily, and Joyce saw her twice a week.

During Joyce's visits with Alice, she observed marked involuntary movement of her right hand that would occasionally strike her face and head. Alice's left arm was stiff across her body and her left hand was in a fist at all times. While these features caught Joyce's attention, she was most enthralled with Alice's bright brown eyes and visual alertness.

Initially, Alice was fearful of Joyce and didn't want physical contact. When she first reached out to touch Alice, a look of terror appeared on her face and she rejected the action. However, a dramatic behavioral change occurred one day when Alice's sister gave Joyce a hug. As Alice carefully observed this gesture of kindness, she knew Joyce was a good person and had Jane's seal of approval. From then on, Alice no longer shunned physical contact from Joyce. Subsequently, when Joyce put her hand on Alice's cheek, she would tip her head and raise her shoulder to squeeze Joyce's hand. They communicated in a special way.

In spite of being nonverbal, Alice enjoyed conversation with Joyce who would talk about subjects of interest. For example, in that Alice grew up on a farm, Joyce talked in detail about farm related subjects (e.g., animals, milking, crops, tractors). During conversation, they maintained eye contact as Alice listened with interest and comprehension. While verbal conversation was one-sided, nonverbal communication took place jointly, and a loving relationship developed.

As do many developmentally disabled individuals, Alice liked music. She had a radio/CD player on her dresser. When she looked in that direction, Joyce knew she wanted the music. Joyce played different types of music to Alice who had a fondness for the country/western type. During the musical interludes, Alice remained content and listened with interest. While Jane was on vacation, Joyce brought a special religious CD composed and sung by a friend of hers. To Joyce's surprise, Alice reacted differently. For the first time, she began to vocalize and moved about in bed to the rhythm of the music. When Jane returned, she wondered what caused all the excitement. Joyce thought it might be a spiritual encounter.

Shortly before Alice's death, Joyce described the moment when her good friend gave a special goodbye. In Joyce's words, "One evening when I went to see Alice, her demeanor was different. However, I couldn't put my finger on it. Knowing how much she liked music, I turned on the CD player and played "Sing Me Home," a song about death and dying. As I sang along, suddenly her left hand (which had always been clenched and immobile) began to shake. I felt she was trying to tell me something. I knelt beside her bed, took her left hand, which was now open, and placed it on top of my hand. It floated. I could move it around. I then took that hand and placed it on my cheek. I asked if she was trying to give me a hug. Her look of loving and compassion said it all. You will never take that look away from me. I think she knew that was the last time we would see each other. She died two days later."

CHAPTER 10

Humorous Incidents with Patients that Involve Family, Hospice Staff and Volunteers

In this section, hospice staff and volunteers share humorous experiences and light moments about patients and families, themselves and even me—big surprise. Some of these stories go back a few years when care and treatment were not as advanced.

"The Accordion Incident"

Sister Milda, a hospice volunteer, just celebrated 50 years of vowed life and still keeps active. She has a terrific sense of humor and a boisterous laugh that reverberates down the hall. She is such a positive influence and picks up everyone's spirits. For some reason, I strike her "funny bone," and she laughs at most everything I say and do. Music is one of Sister's interests and she enjoys playing the accordion to patients and to anyone that will listen. She readily admits she is not an elite musician, in fact far from it. She prefers to play songs in the key of "C," so she doesn't have to hit the black keys. As a novice accordion player, Sister plays her share of "clunkers." However, when disharmonious chords occur, she is unflappable and continues to play.

Claude, a patient with ALS, was Sister's #1 fan. Less-than-perfection did not matter. To him, Sister could do no wrong, and she was the accordion guru. She relished the moments with Claude and enjoyed her ministry of music to him. When she played, his feet took on added strength and rhythmic movement occurred.

When Claude died, his wife requested Sister Milda play her accordion at the funeral. The choice of "Amazing Grace" was in contrast to her signature song, "Beer Barrel Polka." Therefore, she altered her style of play. This was not an easy adjustment. Since there was no one on the dance floor, she struggled a bit. Sister Sue, recognized the challenge that faced Sister Milda, and prayed fervently she would get through the song and preserve its sanctity. God answered her prayer and a miracle occurred. After a few "clunkers," pauses and repeats, Sister delivered a "unique" rendition of "Amazing Grace" that would have pleased Claude.

"The Bedpan Caper"

Sister Sue chuckled as she recalled an incident with the husband of a hospice patient that occurred about 25 years ago. Part of the home training program was orientation on bedpan usage. Sister trained the man to properly position the bedpan so that his wife could use it when needed. This involved how to lift, shift weight and get the appropriate angle to be effective.

The man quickly mastered the technique but had a problem with waste disposal. One day Sister received an unexpected phone call from the man with a strange request. He wanted more bedpans. When Sister inquired why, he reported the three he had were full and in need of replacing. He had placed them outside with the garbage for pickup. The incident prompted Sister to add two segments for bedpan orientation—waste disposal and bedpan maintenance.

"The Lock Out"

Myra, a hospice volunteer for 19 years, recalled a humorous experience with a patient that occurred about 15 years ago. The lady, we'll call Gerty, lived alone and required 24/7 care. Hospice staff and volunteers would care for her in shifts. At the time, Gerty was semi-ambulatory and mentally alert. She possessed a great sense of humor and a feisty spirit. As a prankster, she liked to have fun at the expense of others. For survival's sake, Myra had to keep on her toes. Gerty represented a challenge to say the least.

One day in February, with snow still on the ground, Myra arrived at the home at 7:00 a.m. to relieve staff that worked the night shift. That person left shortly before Myra arrived and locked the door by mistake. Desperate to get in, Myra knocked but didn't get an answer. Perhaps Gerty was in bed she thought. Such was not the case. When Myra peeked in the living room window, Gerty appeared and gazed at Myra with a devilish smile. When Myra motioned to let her in, Gerty, oblivious to the request, gloated and didn't move a muscle.

All Myra's exhortations went unheeded, and she remained outside in the cold. In that she lost the battle, she went to a local gas station and called Gerty's daughter to get a key. With key in hand, Myra returned to the scene, unlocked the door and entered the home. With an ornery grin, Gerty, in jest, asked Myra why she was there.

Not amused, Myra counted slowly to ten and firmly reaffirmed her role. After a few moments, Gerty confessed to the prank but showed no remorse. When asked why she didn't let Myra in the house, with a bit of sadistic pleasure, Gerty responded, "I was having fun watching you." Myra made a cup of coffee, thawed out and planned a strategy to suppress a recurrence—all in the day of a hospice volunteer.

"Poor Choice of Words"

Most everyone experiences moments when an inappropriate word comes "out of the blue" in a conversation for no apparent reason. Recovery from these embarrassments can be problematic and rapport with the unintended receivers challenged. Fortunately, after the initial shock, most experiences turn out humorous for all parties involved and over time, with a few added embellishments, take on a life of their own.

One day such a moment happened at the Home. Kelly, a staff nurse, attended to the needs of a patient who was in discomfort with hemorrhoids. She assured the patient they would treat the condition and said emphatically, "I will bring you some Preparation "H" for your HORMONES," not quite the intended meaning. Silence followed as Kelly made a quick exit from the patient's room to gather her wits. One wonders why that utterance? Was it because "H" begins the word? Perhaps, it was on the mind of the giver and had some personal significance. Whatever the reason, the patient was not offended by the incident and shared in the frivolity. The story continues to be a staff favorite when all share in a good laugh—Kelly included.

"The Wrong Sex"

Warren, a devoted hospice volunteer for over 20 years, related an incident with an elderly patient. Hank, who was well into his 80s, possessed many favorable qualities. However, patience was not one of them. He had a feisty spirit and obstinate demeanor that challenged Warren's role as a caregiver. Hank didn't care how he looked and wasn't concerned about personal hygiene. For Warren to bathe, shave, groom and dress him represented formidable tasks. However, Warren persevered and accepted less than optimal results as major accomplishments. In spite of Hank's negative attitude and noncompliant behavior, Warren acquired affection for him.

One day when unable to visit Hank, Warren called the hospice office to arrange for another volunteer to do the care. The next day Warren returned to determine how the day went with the substitute caregiver. He was apprehensive and expected to see Hank dressed in his usual attire when he looked like a "refugee from a rummage sale." Such was not the case. To Warren's surprise, Hank was immaculately groomed and dressed in a stylish sport shirt and pressed khaki trousers—a real fashion plate.

Warren wondered what had transpired to give Hank a newfound pride in appearance. He got a clue when Hank, who with a look of surprise and disappointment rudely asked, "What are you doing here?" A light came on and suddenly Warren knew why the transformation occurred. It so happened the substitute caregiver was an attractive female who Hank expected to see again. Warren did not fill the bill and was a poor substitute. He took it well and didn't mind to play second fiddle as long as Hank was happy.

"Volunteer Credibility"

On occasion, a patient challenges a volunteer's credibility. To relate a light moment, Fred did not feel volunteers were qualified to care for him in any way. That included transporting him in a wheelchair. Fred had just finished lunch in the dining area and wanted to return to his room.

I accepted the challenge and spent several minutes trying to convince Fred I possessed the necessary skills to perform the task. With some reluctance, he approved. However, it was obvious he had little confidence in me. As I made a special effort to appear self-assured, I released the brakes and then pulled the wheelchair from the table. Next, I carefully turned the chair around. As I exited the dining area, the left wheel clipped the wall that adjoined the living room and we came to an abrupt stop. Fred shook his head in disgust. I no longer had any semblance of credibility. Rather than attempt to remedy the error in navigation, I sought an aide to assist Fred for the journey to his room.

Over time, Fred softened up a bit for he knew how much I cared about him. He even requested that I move him about in the wheelchair. As I skillfully maneuvered the chair through tight quarters, Fred smiled and so did I.

"Undesirable Food Items"

The Home's kitchen staff does a great job to prepare and serve food to patients and families. I'm a testament to Martha's and Myra's culinary delights and have an expanded waistline to show for it. Sometimes unexpected things happen during meals that bring smiles. Once when Roy, a hospice volunteer, removed a patient's tray after dinner, he discovered an unfamiliar container with remnants of a gel-like substance not on the menu. The material had a pungent odor that hardly appealed to the appetite. Roy quickly consulted with staff and an investigation ensued.

The results of the investigation suggested the strange substance to be "bed sore cream." After the discovery, staff fearfully rushed to the patient's side. As they entered his room, he smiled and thanked everyone for the good dinner. His menu that day was Swiss steak, mashed potatoes, pudding and "bed sore cream."

How the latter substance made the food tray remains a question to this day, as does the absence of any intestinal flare-ups on the part of the patient. With the realization that the patient had no discomfort or damage to his body, everyone was relieved and able to laugh. In fact, someone suggested the special cream as a future menu item.

PART 5
Humor in Bereavement

CHAPTER 11

Experiences with Hospice and My Family

General Hospice Experiences

Bereavement counseling is included in hospice programs. Mourning is a natural process that begins with the diagnosis of terminal illness and never ends. The goal of the program is to have the family cope with the loss and make life-altering adjustments that accentuate the positive. Even in death, laughter is encouraged.

While one generally associates sadness and sorrow during bereavement, happy thoughts can also occur as family members recall warm memories of their loved one. Sometimes, these reflections occur when the patient is still alive during the anticipatory grief period. In some instances, these reflections involve humorous incidents that result in laughter. They become vicarious experiences and, for a moment, the family is together again. The positive influence of the departing or departed is present. During these times, it's as if the loved one is saying (quoting Henry Holland), "Laugh as we always laughed at the little jokes we enjoyed together. Play, smile and think of me."

Sometimes children, in their innocence, give remarkable insights that provide comfort for the bereaved. Leo Buscaglia relates an incident of a four-year-old child, whose elderly neighbor had just lost his wife. When the little boy saw the gentleman as he sat outside in his yard, he approached the man and climbed on his lap. When the child's mother asked what he said to the man, he replied, "Nothing, I just helped him cry." I'm guessing he helped him laugh also. That's caring.

Art Buchwald planned his own funeral and invited selected family and friends to deliver eulogies and even suggested what they say. Shortly before his death, he recorded his final message on an answering machine. A humorist to the end, the message said, "I'm Art Buchwald and I just died."

I frequently attend funeral visitations of people I saw as patients. At these times, family and I often share experiences (many on the light/humorous side) about the deceased. During these special moments, smiles often replace tears. It's always a pleasant experience to view the picture displays and videos of the person when healthy and share in their celebration of life.

The full impact of how the death of a loved one affects family evolves over time and not everyone mourns in the same manner. For some, the loss leaves them to mourn without support from others.

To keep busy after the death of a loved one helps occupy one's mind with other things. I recently lost a dear friend who was a hospice patient. Shortly after his passing, his wife got involved with lots of activities outside of the home that she did with supportive friends. In these settings, she was able talk openly about her husband and share fun experiences.

Personal Experiences with My Family

My family continues to mourn the deaths of my in-laws but with happy thoughts and laughter. Over the span of several years, my wife and I were with her parents (Vi and Bud) as their health deteriorated and were present when they died. Vi died first from Alzheimer's disease and Bud two years later from congestive heart failure. They were social people and were never short-changed when it came to having fun. They were inseparable and did everything together. They lived for family and were so proud of their children and grandchildren's accomplishments.

They never missed a high school or college graduation and were present when our daughter graduated from law school. I adored them and was always pleased when they referred to me as their favorite son-in-law. It didn't matter I was the only one.

Our family prayed for Vi's passing in the advanced stages of the dreaded disease. However, when she died, we weren't ready. I don't think you ever are. Fortunately, it didn't take long for our family to resurrect many wonderful memories. After Bud's death, we quickly recalled many fun incidents that the couple did together. The golfing adventure is one of our family favorites.

(Bud and Vi loved to golf and in their senior years often hit the links together. Bud took up the game in early adulthood and Vi in her retirement years. To Bud's dismay, Vi (all of 4 feet—10 inches and 98 pounds) was more athletic and did not take kindly when teased about it. However, I persisted. When they moved to Wisconsin from Connecticut to be with family, Vi was in the early stages of Alzheimer's disease. The game was great therapy for both of them.

I recall one special time on the course that still brings smiles. To create a picture, Bud wore garb that befitted the elite golfer (fancy pants, polo shirt, golf shoes, golf gloves—a real fashion plate). Vi, on the other hand, wore standard outside apparel (shorts, blouse, tennis shoes, no golf gloves). I dropped them off at the golf course and watched as they played the first hole.

Vi insisted that she walk the course while Bud was more content to move about in a golf cart. What a picture it made—a real Kodak moment. Without any fanfare and just one practice swing, Vi drove the ball about 50 yards right down the center of the fairway. Bud complimented her on the good shot. He then proceeded to do several minutes of exercises to loosen up and then took his customary 20 practice swings. He followed with a mighty swing and the ball trickled off the tee about 10 yards to the right. When I told him to keep his eye on the small object, he told me to mind my own business and proceeded to strike it again with a similar result. After he uttered a few expletives, he threw his club farther than he hit the ball. During the escapades, Vi smiled and gave Bud encouragement that he did not appreciate. Didn't she know he was the golfer that had played such prestigious courses as Pebble Beach? With a snicker, I tried to encourage Bud. However, he had enough and was more than ready for the 19th hole.)

In my den, I have a picture of Bud with his golf swing. It's a classic and not the one you'd want to feature in an instructional. A look at the picture always brings a good laugh and conjures up warm memories.

After Vi's passing, Bud loved to spend time in our spacious backyard, filled with flower gardens that he called his "Eden." To him, it was heaven on earth. Often, he would look upward and assure Vi they would soon be together again. Even though age and health limited rigorous yard work, he liked to putter. He loved to trim bushes and was not conservative in his approach. When Bud arrived for an afternoon in the yard, he would go to the closet and get his work hat, work gloves and then pick up his trimmers that were stored in the garage. He would proceed to the back-40 and start to trim every bush in sight. His specialties were honeysuckle and dogwood bushes.

While I would have preferred he trim bushes with a conservative approach, his method of choice was to trim the growth to the ground. In that he received such personal satisfaction as he beautified our estate (at least he thought), I never had the heart to tell him to show more moderation. Even today when I work in the back-40, I feel Bud's presence as I trim the bushes. Those were good times.

While hospice patients frequently have lengthy illnesses and death is imminent, others die suddenly. Such was the case with my brother-in-law Bob, a star athlete and the picture of health, who died of a heart attack at the age of 53. His unexpected death devastated his family, and there was an extended mourning period. While my sister Kathy had terrific family support from her five children who lived close by, it took years for her to talk about Bob without shedding tears. During this time, she was not ready to share humorous incidents about her beloved husband.

Time heals. Now when Kathy's and our families get together, we have happy thoughts about Bob and fun stories abound. Many involve his lack of urgency and a nonchalant attitude when predicaments occurred.

Bob was never in a hurry to get gas for his car. Even when the gauge approached empty, he was convinced he could travel several more miles before he needed to refuel. I was with Bob on three occasions when the car conked out short of its destination. Therefore, I always brought a set of work gloves to prepare for the push. Bob never learned from these experiences and suppressed the concerns of others. When a warning light appeared which signaled a mechanical problem, Bob paid little attention to the alert. In fact, he disguised the evidence by placing masking tape over the flash.

Life is full of balances. Sometimes with the death of a loved one, there is new life. Shortly after my brother-in-law died, my sister and family celebrated the birth of two grandchildren. These gifts strengthened the spirits of Kathy's family and gave hope for the future. From William Blake: "Joy and woe are woven fine; clothing for the soul divine; runs a joy with silken twine."

Closing

In today's age, people are living longer and the quality of life often remains high even in illness. Throughout the book, the uplifting spirit of dying people appears. As one accepts that death is imminent, relationships with family often become stronger. Lines of communication open up and inner most thoughts and feelings revealed. Hospice care provides a wonderful support system for patients and families and tends to bring out the best in everyone. In spite of the patients' deteriorating physical conditions, life continues to have meaning. Though faced with death, these people still desire to be treated the same as before illness. They seek interaction with friends and don't want barriers to affect communication because of illness. Many have "bucket lists" and want to squeeze what they can into living. Often hospice services give them opportunities to achieve these wishes.

As the book suggests, many people with terminal illness still want to have fun, laugh, cry and experience the whole range of emotions. While they live compromised lives, every day is special, and many look forward to a future life. Special moments with family and friends bring smiles and warm memories sustain them. Often their sense of humor never leaves. Throughout the book, humor, often interspersed with song, helps establish rapport, forms connections, provides happy thoughts and reduces communication barriers.

Index